THE STRESS CYCLONE

SUFFER OR EMERGE OUT: THE CHOICE IS YOURS

Dr Rakesh Chopra, a medical graduate and psychologist has done extensive research on 'Corporate Management' through 'Samarpan Yoga' with specialization in the art of Diagnostic Management. His analytical abilities enable him to understand the innermost feelings of executives and provide excellent corporate consultancy. At present, as the Chairman of Institute of Corporate Management, Dr Chopra has been conducting need-based programmes for both individuals and executives in the multinationals, and public and private sectors, based on the principles of 'Samarpan Yoga'.

Mrs Santosh Sharma, a Sanskrit scholar and an excellent counsellor has been involved in research and development on stress eradication and in the area of spirituality. She has done in-depth study of Indian scriptures with special reference to their role in the modern ways of spiritual management. She has the rare ability to take up any assignment on 'Human Resource Development and Management' to the fulfillment of the targeted results.

THE STRESS CYCLONE

SUFFER OR EMERGE OUT: THE CHOICE IS YOURS

DR RAKESH CHOPRA
SANTOSH SHARMA

INSTITUTE OF CORPORATE MANAGEMENT

EXCEL BOOKS

ISBN: 81-7446-231-7

First Edition: New Delhi, 2001

Illustrations
RANA COMPUTERS
Vishnu Garden, New Delhi - 110 018

Cover Photo
Dinesh Chopra

Published by
INSTITUTE OF CORPORATE MANAGEMENT
J-5/42, Rajouri Garden, New Delhi - 110 027
www.stresseradication.com
email: training@stresseradication.com
in association with
EXCEL BOOKS
A-45, Naraina, Phase I,
New Delhi - 110 028

Published by Anurag Jain for Excel Books, A-45, Naraina, Phase-I, New Delhi - 110 028 and printed by him at Excel Printers, C-206, Naraina, Phase-I, New Delhi - 110 028

CONTENTS

PREFACE

"The Stress Cyclone" presents the principles of living, leading to a happy, fresh and peaceful life. This book contributes towards the growth and development of the individuals in gaining excellence in the fulfillment of their responsibilities and the attainment of their goals.

The fast pace at which most people and the growing organizations are functioning these days is putting excessive pressure on senior executives. This pressure is directly affecting their decision making ability and preventing them from regularly updating their relevant concepts for the management of situational change. Thus, this results in low productivity and less profitability.

One of the important reasons for these undesirable results is the lack of proper understanding of winning strategies. The need, therefore, is to understand, formulate, organize and control human activity directed towards specified goals. A winner is a person who has attained peace of mind, a fearless and greedless environment, financial independence, total fitness of body and mind, thus living a dignified and enjoyable social life.

In life people waste a lot of energy because they keep on attempting to manage others and themselves without actually understanding what they are. No doubt human life is a complex phenomenon, still you must direct each and every move towards emerging out of the stress cyclone.

You have all read since your childhood days: "Practice Makes A Person Perfect". Is it true? Perfection is normally understood as a positive expression. But if you keep on practicing wrong methods and that too in the wrong direction, you will be staying far from the positive aspect of perfection.

Additionally, perfection itself is a very complex concept. Perfection generally means you have attained the ultimate. An Olympic champion is normally accepted as perfect in his field. The person could become a champion only after more than a decade's dedicated practice. But what happens the next time? Somebody else comes along and breaks the record. Now, where has that perfection gone?

In life, development is a continuous process. No matter what you accomplish today there will always be scope for further improvement. Perfection is possible only under very selective and specific conditions. Perfection can't be taken as something general. You need to set a specific target with well-defined criteria. Achieving the same can be taken as one level of perfection. If you are keen to attain perfection as a working belief, you must keep on setting and achieving short-term specific goals.

You must plan to move towards excellence. Perfection can be taken as a destination which also has a beginning. Attaining perfection is the end of a specific effort. Once a goal is achieved, only then there is a need to plan the next goal; otherwise there will be an overlapping of many goals, leading to a situation of fluctuating and jerky moments. For further growth you need to plan again and then again. You live in an undefined fear.

While striving for excellence there is no visible end. It is a continuous journey. Once you are on the path of excellence it is smooth sailing. The mind is never blank. Because the track of performance is very clear, the mind remains very fresh and energetic. This way you are mentally prepared to grow every moment.

Normally the word perfection is used only in a positive sense. Excellence is always a positive term while perfection can also be sometimes negative, depending on the track you have chosen. In perfection, you feel happy only at the end and that too if you have achieved as per the set standards. In excellence, you are automatically geared up to gain success and happiness every moment.

Since 1980, through our extensive research it has been established that it is tension which indeed is preventing you in achieving your planned goals. Tension can only be felt and never managed. If you try to manage tension, you only end up feeling frustrated. You must be aware that stress creates tension and tension is an established Silent Killer. It is a living tragedy, when people have physical ailments, every body around is deeply concerned; but when the problem belongs to the mind it is completely ignored. Stress creates tension, and stress must be managed the moment you feel it.

Responsible, ambitious and busy persons experience the effect of stress more. Is becoming ambitious a crime? No, certainly not. But we must know how to understand various life situations in total depth and learn to manage the situation accordingly much before the stress takes its horrifying position.

The Government of India had been focusing on eradicating small pox from the country and now it has been completely eradicated. Now the focus is to eradicate malaria and polio. Similarly now the need of the hour is to eradicate stress too from one's life.

Many people proudly claim that under stress they give their best performance. Ask them a question, is it stress or the concerned job/responsibility coming on top in their priority. This priority is giving them clarity of focus which in turn results in the best performance. If somebody does not know "How to eradicate stress and live a stress free life", this does not mean that stress can not be eradicated.

For family planning one easy and the best method is to educate people on the role of contraception so that the pregnancy does not happen at all. The second method is to set up various MTP centers and conduct abortions which, no doubt, is painful both for the patient and the doctor.

Stress, no doubt, can be managed but it is a painful process. The focus must be on to manage the situation and the stress stands eradicated which is the best and most wonderful solution.

In General Management, normally the focus is on people and results but the self is completely ignored; whereas in stress eradication the initial focus is on the understanding and caring of self, then on people and finally on well directed performance leading to the results.

In the book "The Stress Cyclone", for developing initial understanding of the subject, a set of relevant questions has been provided to help you explore yourself followed by the learning objectives. At the end of the each chapter, for developing the practical-to-implement understanding, subject linked exercises are presented to be explored from your real life situations.

The deeper concept, thus developed, can be easily applied to the management of other situations. So, when life is becoming a stress cyclone, whether you suffer or prefer to emerge out of it, the choice is yours.

DR RAKESH CHOPRA
SANTOSH SHARMA

ACKNOWLEDGEMENTS

We are thankful to the following organizations (to name a few) for giving us an opportunity to interact with their senior executives in group training programmes and individual sessions. Their interaction have helped us understand human behavior and shape the contents as per the need of the hour:

Airport Authority of India, All India Management Association, Amway, Asea Brown Boveri Ltd, BHEL, Carrier Aircon Limited, Central Board of Direct Taxes, Corporation Bank, Denso India Limited, Engineers India Ltd, Escorts Yamaha Motors Ltd, FCI, J K Group, Indian Institute of Petroleum, IFFCO, GAIL, Gillette India Limited, Gujarat Heavy Chemicals Ltd, MTNL, Management Development Institute, Modi Rubber Ltd, National Fertilizers Ltd, NTPC, ONGC, Punjab & Sind Bank, Prakash Industries Ltd, Powergrid Corporation of India Ltd, PNB, Ranbaxy Laboratories Ltd, Rotary International, Siemens Public Communication Networks Ltd, Swaraj Mazda Ltd, The Hindustan Times Ltd, World Health Organization.

Last but not the least, we feel privileged to thank Mr Anurag Jain and his team particularly the editorial team for extending whole hearted support in bringing out this quality publication.

CHAPTER 1

WHAT ARE WE FACING – PROBLEMS OR SITUATIONS?

Explore Yourself

1. Life is full of situations and situations. Are the situations complicated by themselves or do you make them look complicated?
2. Is it the right policy to blame others for your own mistakes?
3. What do you actually want from your life?
4. What should be your practical approach while dealing with your complex problems?
5. What should be your strategy to feel the depth of those situations which you have never experienced in real life?
6. Is there any escape from performance in life?
7. Are you disturbed by the problems or their future consequences?
8. Negative feelings multiply very fast while positive feelings add up gradually. Give your opinion.
9. Has worry got something to do with real life situation or is it only our imagination?
10. Any pleasure in life, once experienced, leaves a restless desire to get it again. Comment.

••••••••••••••••

Learning Objectives

By the end of this chapter, you will be able to :

- feel that the consequences of the problems in imagination lead to discomfort of the mind.
- feel that simple is always powerful while the complicated is bound to be weak.
- know the importance of converting a negative situation into a positive one, the moment it is felt.
- identify logical chain of the Stress Process.

Human life is a complex phenomenon. It is observed that people are largely confused about how to manage their lives effectively. Sometimes, they feel a lot is to be achieved in life and they keep on working very hard but do not feel all that great in the process. At other times they do not want to perform as they feel that nothing is worth achieving. Whether we have some specific aim or no aim at all, still the performance continues. It is wise to get clarity about every activity one is supposed to do.

Human life is full of situations and situations only. In some situations we are thrilled while in others we feel shattered. Whether we welcome them in a happy frame of mind or reject them in desperation, there is no escape from these situations. Something somewhere keeps on happening around us. Situations can be very simple or extremely complicated.

A simple situation practically means no problem. While a complicated one, if not managed effectively in time, will lead to a series of uncomfortable consequences. Our needs and desires to remain comfortable and strong in life. Can we allow ourselves to remain confused and disturbed?

Is The Situation Really Complicated?

Is the situation really complicated in itself or do we make it appear complicated? Had the given situation been complicated in itself then every person would have been equally affected in real life. It is not so. Some people feel highly disturbed in a widely accepted simple situation while others remain very cool and comfortable even in a so called complicated situation.

Some people are afraid of taking an injection while others feel very comfortable even about brain or heart surgery they are planning to undergo. Some people take fifteen to twenty tablets every day quite comfortably while for others even to swallow a small tablet is like experiencing hell.

Depending on one's own practical exposure to various life situations, the reaction is thus positive or negative. Many mature people can behave weak and negative while children can behave constructive and positive. At the young age normally children do not have any serious negative exposure. So the smallest positive and logical exposure will make the child feel and behave in a very strong manner.

Once an eight year old child, while coming from his school, met with an accident. He got an open wound injury in his right knee. His mother was very sensitive by nature. The child realized his responsibility and did not wish to hurt the feelings of his mother. He didn't go home but went to his family doctor and requested, "Uncle, please put stitches on my bleeding wound before my mother comes, otherwise she will cry". The doctor was pleasantly surprised. At that tender age this much was the unexpected understanding and maturity which probably his mother did not have even at her age. After the minor surgery was done, he comfortably informed his mother.

The child, who was normally supposed to suffer and cry, was feeling very balanced and strong while the mother, who was expected to be balanced and caring was giving the opposite image. The doctor is now feeling sandwiched between the two. May be, he feels to be in a position to take the child into confidence for giving the required counselling to the mother.

In this case, the child preferred to make a simple start while his mother was feeling uneasy in her mind. The way we make a start, determines reactions. The more the unsuccessful exposures we have in life the more complicated our life appears. To become strong, it is important to have planned, successful exposures, either as self initiated or provided by our seniors. A pampered child has no exposure of his own, so he feels and behaves very weak when alone. For successfully managing various life situations the age is no bar.

Should We Blame The Situation?

People keep on blaming many of the situations as highly complicated ones; the focus is rarely on understanding and developing the self. We find it comforting to blame others for our own mistakes. It is quite surprising that more of the highly educated people feel miserable in life than the uneducated ones. The vast but hazy exposure, people are getting these days is making them more and more confused and unintelligent. Many of the previous generations' successful business magnates did not receive formal education.

People focus only on gaining maximum knowledge. In the process, they simply ignore getting a deep and clear understanding of the subject concerned. When a person shares his own experiential understanding with us, we just receive it as a knowledge. It does not become our understanding. When we experience that knowledge in the total depth of our respective situations, it immediately becomes our own understanding.

Whenever we plan to manage any situation with our newly acquired knowledge, it looks complicated. The unsaid fact is that we have been going through many similar complicated situations around us, some of which we have also managed. As a result, we confidently start the management of every situation with a complicated approach. This way, we just end up feeling miserable and frustrated. We have put in the best of our efforts and spent lot of our precious energy; still, the results are different from the desired ones.

It cannot be our fault. Centuries ago, the warriors were ruling the masses. So to generate and maintain their own importance, certain intellectuals had made things highly complicated for the common people.

Was There No Choice Left?

Was there really no choice left for us except to follow this confused body of knowledge blindly? On the whole, we lack total clarity of our individual goals. We tend to waste our precious energy in the elaborately explained complicated procedures. The unfelt tragedy of this vast system is that we remain totally unaware of this fact. Generations and generations have been following the life style of their elders. Perhaps we thought there is no other choice and we felt forced from within to adopt the complicated path.

Ask a question to self, "What do I want to get out of my life?" When we keep on asking why, to every question we get the ultimate answer and that would be," I feel good this way. "That leads to the goal of peace and happiness and that's a fact. Whether we define it or it remains undefined, every person born on this earth only wants to be peaceful and happy.

Is peace and happiness possible on this path? Is it advisable to follow the complicated and the difficult to understand approach in managing various life situations or should we simply decide to use our common sense? If the complicated approach seems beneficial, we must adopt the same. But the fact is......

Simple Is Always Powerful While Complicated Is Bound To Be Weak

Due to certain bitter experiences, people become suspicious by nature. They feel that because ten persons have cheated them, so everybody in their life, for sure that is an established cheat. As they could not effectively manage certain situations, they conclude that no solution is available. It is a normal misconception that only self is intelligent and all others are below average. For them, it is difficult to accept anything or anybody at a simple level.

For the respective understanding and management, every situation needs a thorough in-depth assessment. Normally, people attempt to start managing only with a superficial assessment of the situation at hand. They make their ill-equipped and unsuccessful efforts. Then they tend to blame luck for all their failures.

Strategy To Feel The Depth

Be it a game, war, a business proposal or any social function, a well-researched strategy is necessary for its success. Before making a start, we must gain depth on how to play. When we formulate a strategy to play and win a game, we become comfortable and strong to make a start towards victory.

Like a game of chess, before making the next move, we must feel through at least the next seven moves of our opponent. That means accessing his would-be reaction to our move and then our possible reaction to his move and so on ... If we ignore this important strategy then our defeat is almost certain.

"How do we feel the depth of any positive or negative situation?" is a million dollar question. Let us feel the practical and simple-to-implement strategy. Till the relevant depth is felt on the subject, we need to live the consequences in our imagination as if those are already happening. And if we are unable to feel this way then we must learn first, on how to feel the relevant depth. For this experimental plan, let us focus on a hypothetical situation.

Suppose we wish to develop self for feeling the depth about a particular proposed business relation, i.e., relations with the Managing Director of our client organization. We are planning to have a joint collaboration and are scheduled to sign an agreement. If this deal is a balanced one, it can prove to be highly profitable for all times to come. If we are unable to feel future consequences before signing the agreement, it can also prove to be disastrous. Our need, on top priority, is to learn to understand the concerned designated person at the earliest because we cannot afford to delay certain delicate decisions.

Our strategy to gain similar depth is, "Plan to meet ten Managing Directors of some other organizations per day for a minimum of ten days on a courtesy call." In ten days we have felt around one hundred persons. Isn't it? Amazingly, the time taken to feel the depth of the first person was much more than that spent on the last person. Secondly there is a world of difference between the depth we have experienced during our meeting with the first and the last person. At this stage we are very clear about the quality of questions we need to ask because only the correct and relevant information is responsible for the depth required.

Why To Perform?

We wish to develop ourselves. We are keen to justify our day to day responsibilities. We want to help our near and dear ones. We are focusing on gaining name and fame. We love somebody to the extent of showering all our resources or we hate someone to the extent of taking fatal revenge. Even if we have no plans to achieve anything specific at all, we simply cannot escape actions (conscious or even at sub-conscious level). There is no choice. The voluntary activity where we have a choice is also directing us to do something.

The path of escapism is simply not possible. On our part any attempt to escape voluntary or involuntary actions will only give a feeling of frustration.

No Escape

Similarly, when you are confronted with a realistic situation, there is no escape. A temporary escape is only a diversion for the time being. It may give a short lived satisfaction as in the old "Pigeon and cat story" wherein the pigeon closes its eyes when confronted by a cat, imagining that the cat has gone away. Till today the cat is still smiling at the pigeon's escapist approach. The fact is that the total escape is neither practical nor possible. Those who attempt to escape can never be peaceful as the relevant pressures keep on increasing.

No Escape

In any given situation you are bound to take a decision and perform accordingly. Non-performance will also lead to some situation which needs a further decision. Obviously, escape is again not possible. According to the understanding and depth in one's life the same situation will mean differently to different people. The less depth we have in life, the more disturbed we will be. Of course, material resources are important but only these are not enough to generate peace and happiness.

Investment Capacity

Any person who has lots of money may not have the mind to invest lavishly. His visible focus is to collect and possess money. At the most he only behaves like a caretaker. At the same time, a person who is not rich can plan to invest even bigger amounts beyond his present capacity with full ease. A person who has the mind to invest, knows the value of money.

For example, if two persons have lost rupees ten thousand each on the same day they will react to it differently. For one person this loss may mean nothing because he is in the habit of giving this amount to various charitable institutions as a donation every now and then. He also feels comfortable in entertaining his guests in the five-star culture. He knows the difference between an investment and wasteful expenditure. He is not possessive of money but knows how to earn money and spend it wisely. He believes in living in the present. He is not disturbed at the said loss but is focusing his energy on how to generate more funds.

But for the other person it is his salary for the month. He has a limited exposure to life. For him it is indeed a difficult situation. If by chance on the same day, he wins a lottery of twenty thousand rupees, this situation no longer remains difficult for him. Then he becomes immediately comfortable. In life, whenever you are unable to manage a difficult situation, you normally refer to that as a problem.

Consequences Are The Problem

In fact, the problem is not the realistic loss of money but the consequences attached to it. How to pay the rent of the house? The children will demand money to pay the school fees, otherwise the teacher will ask them to keep standing in the class or the principal may take a decision to strike off their names from the school. His ailing wife needs medical care. How can she be admitted to a nursing home? How will he manage to pay her medical bills? Next week is the marriage of a cousin. Oh yes, there is a contributory party in the office too. He will feel highly embarrassed to face all those people who will come to collect monthly bills.

If his boss immediately sanctions him an advance of the same amount, to be returned in the next five years, again there is no problem. Loss of money or unacceptable action is not the problem. Even on the death of somebody close people normally weep and feel disturbed over the loss of those certain benefits they were getting from the deceased. Only the consequences are the problem and not the loss of money or the person.

Feeling of Fear

Normally, whenever one is unable to find a viable and easy-to-implement solution to one's problems, a feeling of fear comes into the mind. Nothing untoward has happened but the person is literally trembling from within as if he has been caught red handed and fully exposed. A feeling of unmanageable guilt enters his already disturbed mind. He starts giving irrelevant justification to what he feels would have happened.

People around him have a specific image about his personality and behaviour. They feel confused about what he is talking. They have never experienced him in that state of mind. Their negative and confused reaction to what he is doing is quite natural. An ill conceived negative chain starts in the understanding of that person and people in his circle. Now something visibly negative has happened in the reaction of others. Because of this chain reaction, he further starts getting a feeling that now almost everybody knows the worst that has happened to him.

He makes it a point to avoid all those concerned people and situations. He withdraws into his own shell, feeling as if nobody understands him. All this completely blocks his mind. He feels very lonely and totally cut off from the world and his surroundings. The tragedy is - as yet, nothing negative has happened and the poor fellow is feeling miserable. He is losing control over himself and can not manage as desired. Perhaps he is not aware that......

Negative Feelings Multiply Very Fast While Positive Feelings Add Up Gradually

Once the negative process starts, the situation simply goes out of control. Many people claim and act to remain positive but it takes time before they become fully positive. Because one is trained to live and accept the negative, it actually becomes very difficult for a person to initiate the constructively positive track.

Let us take the case of an animal. While going on a lonely road, a person comes across a dog staring at him. The immediate reaction is that this dog might bite him. Surprisingly the dog also is developing similar feelings while looking at the person. Both the parties start with the same negative feelings. In the process of defending, both prepare to attack each other. As they come closer, the dog starts barking and the person picks up a stone. Throughout, both are under the firm grip of panic. The person throws the stone at the dog, in response the dog jumps and literally bites the person.

This never happens if the person does not start the first negative feeling. We can just pass by the dog and the dog is equally comfortable. When we are not sure of self and attempt to start with a positive note, it requires a lot of courage to pass through that area smoothly.

Fear – Worry – Fear .....

As time passes one feels future consequences in one's imagination. At a very fast pace one is coming under the grip of fear. Initially, there is a small bout of fear. This fear is just a reflex action from a very weak and negative base. It is not very difficult to come out of that state. The negative process has just begun, so initially there is a feeling that fear is going away but the fact is it is just diluting its effect temporarily. One remains in the grip of a mild attack of fear known as WORRY.

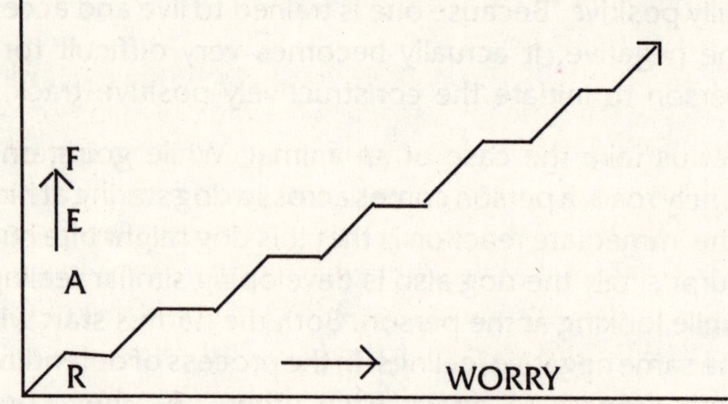

When the state of worry continues for some time, the negative feelings silently keep on multiplying and there is one more attack of fear. Again, the intensity of fear becomes diluted leading to the state of worry again. The fear and worry supplement and complement each other. This chain "fear-worry-fear" goes on becoming more and more powerful.

Only In One's Imagination

Worry exists only in one's imagination and never in reality. The grip of fear becomes very powerful with continuous multiplication of negative feelings and one accepts the negative imagination as something real. It is our choice to feel anything in imagination. We can feel positive or negative. The reality is that we have the freedom to experience any feeling. Normally we tend to start from the negative. It looks that the negative is bound to happen – "I am not so lucky to receive the positive." We have forgotten all the positive in the past but the negative remains very much alive in our memory.

In reality, nothing has happened. Sometimes a person will mistake a rope for a snake in the dark. Similarly one is feeling self generated highly charged, but baseless, negative imagination as real and gets panicky. It is impossible to fight with nothing in front. The more efforts one makes to fight, the more frustrated one becomes. It is an unmanageable clash of imagination with reality thus leading to a disturbed mind.

Let us take the situation of a happily married young couple. The husband is normally reaching home at 6 PM on the dot. The wife eagerly starts waiting for him for the evening tea much earlier than that. One day the bell does not ring at 6 PM as expected. She starts feeling uncomfortable. Some irrelevant doubts enter her mind.

May be he has been attracted to some other girl. No, no, it is not possible God cannot be cruel to me. The time now is 8 PM. Still he has not come. Many ideas keep on disturbing her. Nothing comes clearly to her mind. The door bell has rung two to three times in between but it was somebody else. She feels disappointed.

She suddenly realizes, "Oh yes, it could only be an accident." She feels horrible from within. She starts perspiring heavily. It cannot happen. I am worshipping God everyday. God is very kind to me. She starts her evening prayers. Now it is 10 PM. Still there are no signs of his coming home. Not even a message.

12
9
3
6

What could have happened? It is certainly a very serious accident. May be he is.............. No, I do not agree with this feeling of mine. Only an year ago we got married. It is not possible but this much late.... may be he is no more.

It is 12 midnight and suddenly the door bell rings. She trembles from within so is unable to move. How can she open the door? The bell rings again and again. With lot of difficulty she opens the door and is deeply shocked .... to see her husband alive. In her imagination she had accepted that the worst had already happened. So it was difficult for her to come out of that situation. She was totally numb for a couple of minutes..

It is indeed an unmanageable heavy clash of reality with imagination. The circumstances over the years have trained the human mind to escape from the present. People can only predict the future but nobody can ever be sure of the future. The negative chain in our imagination is so strong that even the strongest person also feels trapped and weak. He feels compelled to escape from reality.

Whenever we accept in imagination that the worst has already happened then any advice from any body carries no meaning. The fact is that advice is coming from the present base while imagination has gone far beyond the present. The two do not match. The badly trapped person strongly feels that there is no solution to his situation. But in a way this is very much true. There is no solution to what does not exist.

Towards Stress

It's obvious that fear, along with worry, builds up an increasing pressure in the imagination. Imagination is very powerful. We can give any track to our mind and it runs on that negative or positive track accordingly. Imagination is mostly an emotional state of mind so, it can easily divert a person on the unrealistic negative path. Because the speed of mind in that direction is increasing constantly, it becomes difficult for anybody to stop that negative path. Under these circumstances the control becomes almost impossible.

As negative feelings multiply very fast the person tends to link the ultimate negative point with the starting point. Its a mistaken thought when one feels that the same point has just been magnified but the fact is, he has gone far away from where he began. In the beginning he also had a positive choice but now the negative has overpowered him. The negative grip has become very strong. When imagination appears close to reality it attains a level of pressure which cannot save the mind from disturbance.

This highly charged negative imagination puts a pressure on the person called as STRESS. This pressure can also be because of any direct problem being faced in the present. If we limit the problem only to the present situation, the required control remains. Again at sub-conscious level, one starts feeling the future consequences. Any person under stress is not feeling normal and balanced. Is this pressure life long? You must have experienced that....

Nothing But 'Change' Is Permanent

So this highly uncomfortable state also needs an escape. Let us understand this concept with the help of an inflated balloon. We can compare the balloon with a human being. The pressure you put on the balloon is the stress which leads to changes on in the balloon. Newton's Third law of motion states "Action and reaction are equal and opposite".

The actual pressure we are exerting on the balloon will have an equal and opposite reaction. The body of the balloon will show some changes and even the inside pressure will be affected. Stress has an equivalent effect on the human mind and body. Before actual pressure is exerted on the mind a feeling of fear may come about the harmful effects of that stress. Reaction also starts in one's imagination.

If the strongly negative situation is accepted in one's imagination there will be an equal and opposite reaction as that of the actual. As long as the negative remains only in imagination, the harmful effects are not unbearable but the moment it becomes the reality, escape is very difficult.

Generating Tension

As we understand, stress generates a pressure within the mind, commonly known as TENSION. The balloon also, in that state of tension, does not look appealing. Depending on the level of stress, tension builds up accordingly. The more the stress, more is the tension leading to more discomfort. We do not want to live on

Generating Tensions

uneasy life. It is shocking to know that people love to live in tension. They feel there is no other choice. If they are not aware of the solution that does not mean that it does not exist. They prefer to remain blind to this fact. As if they have married 'worry' which has become a part of life and tension is their own baby who needs proper pampering. How can they live without it?

Many people want only a male child. When a female child is born, instead of happily accepting they tend to blame the mother or even God. Their whole life is filled with hatred and suffering. They associate a male child with a false feeling of status. He can be a would-be partner in business, a caretaker in old age or even keeps the family name alive. The male child, at the time of need, may not give the ultimate comfort.

The focus of majority of people is only on feeling the depth of pleasures. It is very important to know and feel the difference between pleasures and happiness. Worldly pleasures are always short lived while the happiness can be permanent. In this world every material pleasure once experienced will make us more and more restless to experience it again.

Any pleasure that leads to sufferings, cannot be a pleasure and is far from happiness. We must focus on peace and happiness. If we do not know the right path towards a life full of peace and happiness, it does not mean that the option of the right path does not exist. Tension, once experienced, will initiate multiplication of negative feelings.

The Visible Strain

The effect of stress on the body is called as STRAIN. When we tell somebody not to over strain, we generally refer to physical aspect only. Whenever the mind is tense, the muscles are equally affected. The strained expressions are clearly visible on the face and other parts of the body. We have a limited store of energy and it is very precious. When the muscles are involved energy is diverted towards the body muscles and is wasted. We feel weak and lethargic.

Just before any examination, when not fully prepared, people normally tremble. The focus is on the body and is a true expression of strain. Examination is not only academic. At every stage in life every situation is indeed an examination. Many a time the situation at hand does not need any specific physical involvement but the stress that leads to tension will have an equal effect on the body as strain. The body muscles need energy and in the process we feel physically weak.

Similarly the mind also needs energy to remain tense. Here the energy is diverted towards the mind and is again wasted. As a result we experience an overall fatigue. As the negative multiplies very fast, we are moving towards an undesirable serious situation of continuously increasing tension and strain.

Let us learn to arrest the negative, the moment it comes and convert that into the positive, so that the most precious step, i.e., our initiative is never blocked.

UNMANAGEABLE SITUATION

PROBLEM

FEAR

WORRY

STRESS

TENSION STRAIN

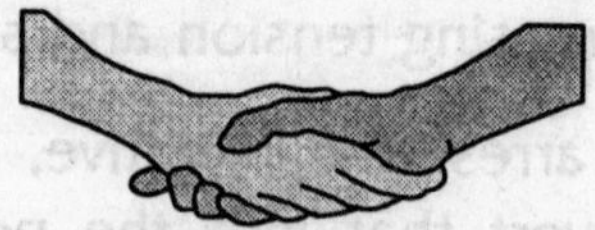

Purpose

To understand the strategy to feel the depth of those important situations which you have never experienced in real life.

What To Do

After feeling your ultimate goal in life, identify the areas where you need to feel the depth for your development and control.

Purpose

To understand that negative feelings multiply very fast while positive feelings add up gradually.

What To Do

Identify ten situations from your past where your initial negative feelings had multiplied in totally irrelevant directions. Feel the loss which could have been avoided.

Purpose

To know the importance of converting negative into positive the moment it is felt.

What To Do

Identify ten negative situations from self and others' experiences. Plan how will you convert these negatives into positives.

CHAPTER 2

LEADING TO THE CYCLONE WITHIN

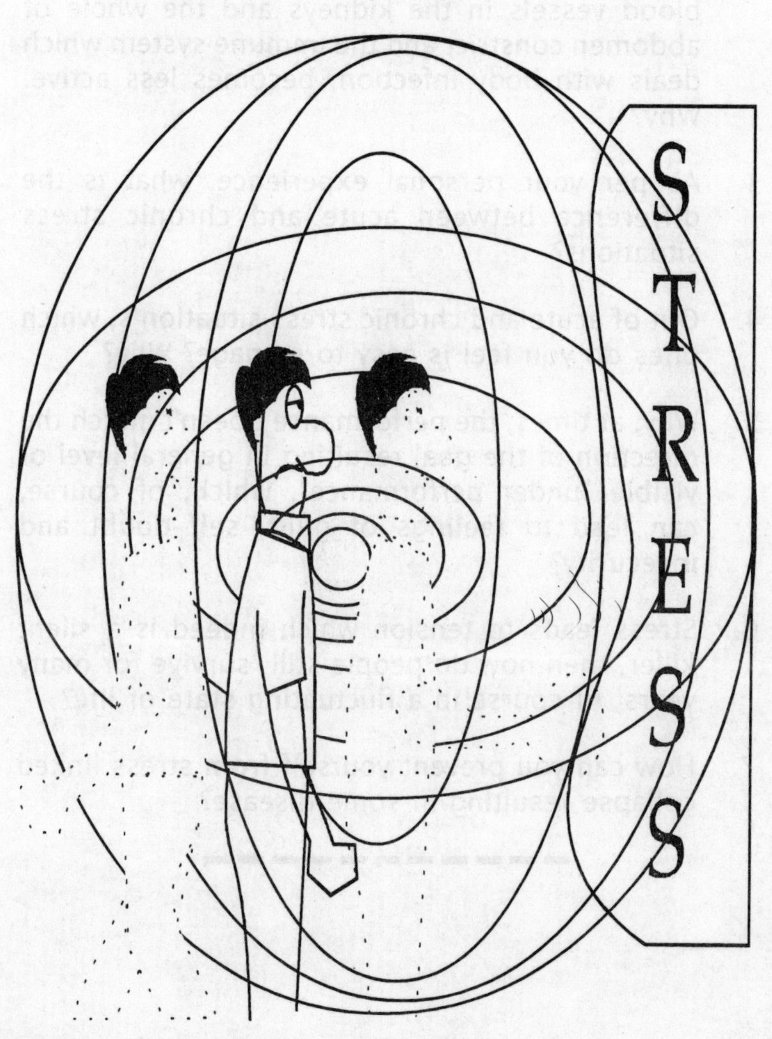

Explore Yourself

1. While encountering a stressful situation do you feel like fighting or escaping?

2. When a typical situation converts into a stress cyclone, the digestive system slows down or even stops altogether, the salivary glands dry up, the blood vessels in the kidneys and the whole of abdomen constrict and the immune system which deals with body infection, becomes less active. Why?

3. As per your personal experience, what is the difference between acute and chronic stress situations?

4. Out of acute and chronic stress situation's, which ones do you feel is easy to manage? Why?

5. Why, at times, the performance doesn't match the direction of the goal resulting in general level of visible "under performance", which, of course, can lead to feelings of guilt, self-doubt and insecurity?

6. Stress leads to tension which indeed is a silent killer, then how do people still survive for many years, of course in a fluctuating state of life?

7. How can you prevent yourself from stress linked collapse resulting in some disease?

Learning Objectives

By the end of this chapter, you will be able to :

- get clarity that the fight or flight mechanism is the beginning of the stress cyclone and if not managed in time, can cause great damage to the body and mind.
- understand and manage the adaptation stage of body's reaction to the stress cyclone.
- feel the possible dangers of the exhaustion stage and body's reaction to the stress cyclone.

The human body needs total harmony. Whenever there is a threat to the body some automatic defence mechanism is always available to counter the threat. Whether the demands on body are generated internally or externally, the body strives to be efficient constantly. It further strives to attain an equilibrium in which the various bodily systems work harmoniously in response to the demands made on them. When such demands become potentially harmful to the body, they are generally called stress factors.

These range from such obvious stimuli as excessive noise, heat or cold, overwork, overburdening, family or business commitments and even some well defined or undefined internal worries such as imagined threats or fears that result from prolonged anxiety. If we can identify how our body will react to stress then the possibility of managing it becomes more clear.

No two persons will react in a similar manner to the same situation. The reaction depends on one's exposure in the past and training to understand and manage the future. Accordingly, the reaction to these stress factors is different. No doubt people wish to remain calm and happy but that is not possible as they have developed wrong or negative habits to deal with every situation they come across.

Fight Or Flight Reaction

Based on one's personality, whatever the stress factor, the body's response follows a predictable pattern. This response has been called the "fight or flight" reaction because the body is preparing either to fight or to run away. It is the beginning of stress cyclone. Along with a rapid increase in metabolism, hormonal, physiological and biochemical changes take place instantaneously.

During the "fight or flight" phase the muscles of the body become tense, as if preparing to save the cyclone. The part of the brain which is called hypothalamus is a coordinating centre for multitude of body functions not normally under voluntary control. It receives an alarm message and calls into play the hormonal function of the master gland, the pituitary. The hormones produced by the pituitary gland now mobilize other areas producing hormones, notably the adrenal glands, which release adrenaline and noradrenaline to keep the "fight or flight" reaction going. These bring about a series of physiological changes that are essential for any specific activity to take place in response to the stress stimulus.

For proper functioning muscles need glucose. The liver responds to this by releasing some of its store into the bloodstream, which carries it to the muscles. Glucose has to be transformed into energy so the blood also carries the necessary oxygen. Thus heart has to pump harder to make blood flow to parts where it's most needed which leads to a rise in blood pressure. Breathing becomes faster, so the lungs can take in extra oxygen.

As the amount of blood in the body is limited, it has to be diverted to the priority areas - muscles, heart, lungs, kidneys and the brain. Consequently, there's a temporary "shutdown" in other areas; for example, the digestive system slows down or stops altogether, the salivary glands dry up, the blood vessels in the kidneys and the abdomen constrict, the immune system, which deals with body infection, becomes less active.

All this is appropriate if the stress factor is best dealt with by physical action. For instance, if the source of stress is a hostile dog running towards you, you'll need all the help your body can give, to run fast as you dash for safety. Once you're safe, the body swiftly reverses the process and no harm is done.

But today, physical responses such as running away may not be appropriate. For how long and how much can we do it? When the whole complex mechanism is brought into play repeatedly, our body and mind finds difficulty in resolving stress. Acute situations may seem easy to manage but obviously in chronic situations ....

Fight Or Flight Mechanism Can Cause Great Damage To The Body

Aithough the "fight or flight" reaction has been a part of man's survival kit throughout history and has enabled those equipped with the best response to survive, it hasn't adapted itself to the more subtle forms of stress reaction required in a modern competitive society.

Adaptation Stage

When stressful situations occur repeatedly over a long period without resolution, a second stage of stress - the adaptation stage - is reached. Many of the changes that took place in the acute "fight or flight" phase become chronic - they take place all the time - so that they're working against, rather than for us. The negative under these circumstances is becoming permanent.

The problem of high blood pressure (hypertension) becoming permanent is greater because of the compulsive maintenance of constricted blood vessels. Even circulatory problems involving the heart may begin to appear. When stress arousal occurs our digestive system also functions more slowly or stops altogether. There is a tendency in the adaptation or chronic phase to develop such conditions as stomach or duodenal ulceration, colitis, diarrhoea or constipation. Chronic muscular tensions can also produce a multitude of musculoskeletal aches and pains as well as severe headaches. The sustained or repetitive stress stimulus impairs the working of the body's defence mechanisms, which makes infection and allergic symptoms more likely. The likelihood of nervous symptoms such as nervousness and phobias also becomes greater.

The fact remains that one is mentally used to a previous specific and established system of operation. During the adaptation phase there is a dramatic contrast between what the individual intends to achieve and what the now malfunctioning system is capable of achieving. All planning is done based on the past system while there is a totally unmatching present base for performance.

When goal and performance do not match, there is a general level of "under performance", which can, of course, lead to feelings of guilt, self-doubt, insecurity, etc. Under these circumstances the effort put in is much less than the effort required. Intentions are clear but confusion prevails throughout performance. Visible job performance declines, libido will often disappear and personal relationships are strained.

All of this creates further stress at a time when the person is least able to cope with it. One feels confused about what is happening. By the time he is in some position to identify what has happened, more stress has already set in, leading to more confusion. There is an overlapping of confusing situations and one finds oneself in its firm grip. Inspite of repeated efforts the results are not coming. Ultimately, one feels compelled even to accept that there is no other choice for him. He has to live his life in misery only. In the past, he could do the jobs with great ease, now look impossible to him. One always feels ready with some irrelevant excuse like, "I have now grown old. My father is not with me to give me support. Technologies have changed. My children don't listen to me," and so on.

Adaptation Stage

Just how long this phase can go on without a major mental or physical breakdown depends upon many factors. Some of these can be inherited constitutional factors; basic health habits such as diet and exercise; and the degree of emotional support provided by the family and friends.

The adaptation phase can last 10, 15 or 20 years, or it may be brief, depending on many different factors, such as the ones mentioned above. When health is properly maintained with a balanced diet and regular exercise, human resistance is increased and the same force of stress will not be harmful to the same extent . Anybody who has a constant emotional support from family members and close dependable friends preserves a strong mental base.

Similarly, people who have attained spiritual depth of life are not moved by any amount of pressures from any source. If the positive is strong and dominant, the negative automatically tends to disappear.

Exhaustion Stage

Nobody wants to feel exhausted but the focus on managing and coming out of the worsening adaptation stage is totally missing. No solution is possible without initiation of action in the right direction. Sometimes, people are aware of the source of resources to help them feel comfortable but they are reluctant to make an effort to get them for their benefit. Their hesitation becomes a curse on them. If action can be taken at the adaptation stage to alter either the stress factors or the reactions to them, then the final exhaustion phase can still be avoided.

However, if action is not taken before the adaptation phase ends then the exhaustion phase follows. At this stage the body is no longer in a position to cope; so it collapses into disease of one form or another. Once the disease sets in, the resistance of body and mind is lowered, thus inviting various dangers.

Being able to recognize the signs and symptoms of stress and knowing how to escape from the vicious acute adaptation-exhaustion spiral is, therefore, of the utmost importance.

Purpose

To get clarity that the fight or flight mechanism can cause great damage to the body and mind.

What To Do

Make a list of ten past situations when you had experienced fight or flight reactions. Which way can you plan to manage similar situations again?

Purpose

To develop understanding as to how to manage the adaptation stage of body's reaction to stress.

What To Do

Plan to meet ten persons who are undergoing the adaptation stage. What will be your advice to these persons?

CHAPTER 3

THE LIFE WE LIVE

Explore Yourself

1. Challenge is normally taken as a feeling of guaranteed success which prevents the mind from becoming negative. There can also be a false feeling of this guaranteed success leading to unexpected consequences. Give your opinion.

2. In life, experience alone can't make you an authority on Stress Management. Should you learn to simply ignore, overcome or accept stress as a part of living or identify planned efforts to manage it?

3. If the choice is to select only one. Would you prefer to live with acute stress situations or the chronic stress situations? Why?

4. Which way would you plan to improve the quality of your life?

5. Do you really want to manage stress or are you too much identified with the stressful life style?

6. In your surroundings identify the sources from where the stress comes in your life.

7. In your opinion what is the reason that inspite of their best management skills, many visibly successful people in life are also not peaceful and happy?

Learning Objectives

By the end of this chapter, you will be able to :

- feel that accepting stress as a challenge may not give you positive and balanced feelings.
- know the importance of acute and chronic stress responses in the life you live.
- understand how to improve quality of life.
- develop understanding on various stress factors of your life.

Throughout the world, stress has literally become a household word. Even a child today talks about stress. How does it affect us? How can we recognize stress in our life? Sometimes, without understanding the true meaning of stress, we often say, " Put more stress on this issue " or " Don't put stress. " This indeed is a planned action within our control. It is basically focusing on an identified force.

Let us see what the word 'stress' stands for in our mind. Is it something positive or the beginning of an extremely negative track or is it just neutral? If it is positive there is nothing to worry about. It is a moment of celebration. But if it is negative, it can prove to be delicate and dangerous. Better be careful!

By now, we know that negative feelings multiply very fast and must be tackled the moment they are felt; otherwise, the most fatal is destined to happen. Even if the so called, most balanced personalities once go negative, it becomes very difficult for them to return to the positive. Should I live with the feeling that I am the most intelligent person in this world, that I can and I will manage every odd situation of my life? Or should I consider myself as one of the countless people in this world who are committing mistakes every day?

Inspite of the fact that the negative aspect of stress can be dangerous, majority of people take stress as something positive. They feel that the negative will not happen to them, it is meant only for others. Is it ever possible ? Every person in life has encountered various "difficult" and "not so difficult" problems without escape. It is just a reflection of the same old feeling " People die but I will not ". We are never prepared for our own death or any other extreme negative to happen to us.

Is Stress A Challenge?

The positive aspect of stress is normally considered as a challenge which fills people with the energy to perform. Challenge gives a feeling of guaranteed success and prevents the mind from becoming negative. Challenge is always an emotional expression. It is not an asset as it is generally taken to be but, if not properly handled, can be easily converted into a permanent liability. There can also be a false feeling of the so called guaranteed success leading to unexpected consequences.

If the feeling of challenge is not logically well defined and accepted then, during performance, the track of success can be easily lost. Even a slight deviation at the initial stage will take the person far away from the planned destination in the long run. There is a delicate but variable line of demarcation between the expected positive and visible negative aspects of stress. Our emotional track keeps on fluctuating because of the invisible and uncontrollable entry of certain problematic situations. This automatically disturbs the level and position of this line. As this line does not remain stable, we can't be sure of positive outcome.

People normally feel that to perform, certain amount of pressure is always required. Pressure is an emotional expression but when it is logically directed it becomes a force which is positive. Force has a penetrating effect on the well defined target towards success. But it again should be relevant to the need. More force applied than the required amount, can even prove to be disastrous or can lead to a lot of wastage.

Demands Of Life

Stress has many meanings, but most people take stress to be the need of life. Technically, these demands are called "stress factors" and the actual wear and tear on our bodies is the stress. The demands or challenges of life can come from people and events around us, as well as from our inner thoughts and struggles. When these demands increase, people often feel that they are under excessive stress.

One of our goals is to present better ways not only to learn to live with stressful situations but also to find more enjoyment in meeting and logically mastering the challenges of our changing world. Change indeed is a supporting part of our life . We might feel bored if we were forced to spend our days sitting in an easy chair. We are bound to face many stressful situations every day. At the same time we need to live life successfully. We must identify our stress responses and then decide to learn tested techniques to deal with them. When we live successfully in a stressful world, we will be neither over stressed nor under stressed. This neutral but visibly non-negative situation of life will keep us on the track of peace and happiness.

Most people are not aware of their minute-to-minute stress responses. Our responses to stress situations are not techniques and concepts learned by feeling the depth of life. By and large, these are results of trial and error methods. Experience alone cannot make us an authority on Stress Management. For better or worse, we learn to ignore, overcome, or accept these as part of living. What are these important stress responses?

Acute Stress Responses

At times, we are all too aware of how stress affects us. Have you ever felt that your stomach was " full of butterflies "? May be you had a lump in your throat, or your chest felt tight. Perhaps your pulse raced and your heart pounded. You may have felt pain in your neck and shoulders because of tension.

We have all heard of "Examination Fever". Is the fever real or the unbearable effect of stress? We face some very difficult situations which can be a job interview, a school or college examination, appearance in a court of law or even encountering a typical family conflict situation. The body temperature remains normal but the body doesn't. One has bodyaches, feels nervous throughout, complains of having diarrhoea, doesn't like the slightest noise and even starts blaming every body for every fault of his own.

During such a situation, may be we felt sweaty or all wound up; thoughts may have raced through our mind. But when someone asked us a question, the mind went blank. We felt totally confused as to what has happened to us. We have been proved to be very intelligent at number of occasions. We have handled many debates and won many gold medals. Many people at this time blame the growing old age and accept that the memory has faded away. Once such negative thoughts occur they multiply very fast.

Can we remember getting upset and having any of these responses? Most of us have experienced some of these feelings at one time or another.

Chronic Stress Responses

The acute stress response normally does not disturb people much because they get back to normal soon. The acute stress responses are physical or behavioural level warning signs. When stress is unduly prolonged and becomes chronic, the short term warnings become more serious stress responses. To overcome the harmful effects of stress, some people work longer and

FEELING BLANK

harder but actually become less productive. For many, the words " I don't have time because I am surrounded by so many important assignments " become a way of life. They feel proud of this kind of status but the fact is, it is an attempt to escape.

Dangerous stress disorders can follow changes in the way we feel and act. As an ultimate effect, some people become withdrawn or depressed. They feel afraid of coming out of their shell. The pressures are increasing moment by moment and time is running out. The situation is going from bad to worse.

Smoking and drinking may become persistent problems. One's sexual life may suffer. Pain associated with headaches, arthritis and other chronic diseases may increase. Some people eat more and gain weight, while others eat less and lose weight. Sleeplessness and over sleeping may become problems. Day dreaming and difficulties with concentration are common. Feelings of suspiciousness, worthlessness, inadequacy or rejection may become prominent.

Too many of us have some of these experiences at too many times. We find ourselves anticipating the worst and being unduly nervous before anything has happened. We may not recognize how our personality has changed. Even if the changes are pointed out to us, we may not believe we have changed.

A wealthy industrialist was blessed with a son after ten long years of marriage. He had done a lot of hard work to become rich. He was feeling proud of himself for all the achievements of his life. He was very keen that his only son should become his successor. He must take over his entire business empire. Surprisingly, his son was least interested in business. To generate his interest he planned to give him exposure to all the luxuries. Any desire he expressed was immediately fulfilled. The way the son grew up, his word became the law. He never experienced any problem.

One day the father decided to give the business exposure to his son. He was made to visit the office and the factory. There he came across a number of persons who were suffering from poverty, disease or various business and family conflicts. He had never experienced any negative in life. He felt disturbed. He went on a long drive to find an escape from his disturbed feelings. Far away from his place he met with an accident. The angry crowd surrounded him. There was nobody to defend him. He felt highly uncomfortable. He also accepted in his imagination that the worst was going to happen. He went into deep shock. He felt lifeless and the father was helpless.

Notice that no matter where stress comes from, if the short term effects occur intensely and frequently, the long term costs are the same - the quality of life suffers. What is the benefit of living the life without the life itself in it? Perhaps we can't change circumstances or our doing something around us may not be practically possible. On the other hand, if we increase and refine our skills of understanding, life and health actually improve.

Improve Quality of Life Refine Your Understanding Skills

We normally invite problems in life because of lack of understanding of various life situations. First of all we must evolve a strategy to understand ourselves, others and every situation of life, then gain competence and, with regular controlled practice, develop skill. This way our understanding skills will be gradually refined and quality of life improved.

Where Does Stress Come From?

We define stress factors broadly as external demands of life or the internal attitudes and thoughts. Stress factors can include conflict with spouse, traffic jams, pollution in the city, that fifth cup of coffee, the pushy salesman who will not take no for an answer, or the angry boss. Stress factors can also include the work that never seems to get done, the children who never seem to obey, or the way some people put themselves deep down for their shortcomings. Notice that some of these stress factors come from our unavoidable surroundings and others from our inner struggles. Some stress factors come from both sources.

Many elements contribute to stress factors becoming stressful. There are certainly individual differences among us. "You can't make a racehorse out of a turtle." How much control we have over the stress factors and whether we feel we have a choice in our exposure to them will determine our response. If we "have to" work late because the boss "ordered us," for example, we will respond differently than if we "choose to" work late because we wanted to finish the project and take the weekend off. The fine compatibility between a person's background, aspirations, interests and his/her work will also determine how stressful the work seems.

Focussing on stress factors in different categories will help us become more aware of the varieties of stress in our life. As we feel the brief descriptions that follow, imagine an average day and consider how each stress factor may be reducing our enjoyment of life.

Emotional Disturbances

Emotions are responsible for all the pleasures and the sufferings of life. Only emotions make us feel on top of the world and emotions alone make us feel shattered. May be we are not aware that human emotions are within our own control. If we don't exercise control over any project then loss is almost guaranteed. Many of the emotional stress factors we experience are not even relevant to our respective lives.

Emotional stress factors include the fears and anxieties with which we struggle: Can we prevent a nuclear war? What if we run out of petrol? What if I lose my job? What will happen if the government changes? Additional emotional stress factors include worrying about unpaid bills, or taking an examination etc.

The messages we silently give ourselves about our actions and the actions of others are also emotional stress factors. Telling ourselves how "awful" we are going to do in some activity is an emotional stress factor that may lead to poor performance. On the other hand, consistently denying that we need to be prepared and "do our homework", may also be an emotional stress factor and can lead to failure. Both being afraid of tomorrow and procrastinating today's activities can trigger stress responses.

Each individual has a unique set of emotional stress factors. Some of them may seem contradictory. One person may not be concerned if bills are paid late but may be very concerned if his girl friend is not on time. Another person may be very upset about paying a bill late but hardly concerned if his girl friend is not on time.

Family Responsibilities

Interactions with our family members can be stressful because of the rising conflicts in the system. Each person's demands are increasing day by day. Over the years, family structure also has been changing drastically. The institution of marriage was once a strong, supportive force that could help family members cope with other stress factors. Now, the number of marriages ending in divorce is on the rise and many children born in the last decade will spend at least a part of their youth in homes with only one parent.

Besides the conflicts, the families go through various stages of stress even otherwise. The birth of a child places new demands for adaptation on a family. Immediately after birth the normal sleep for the parents is no more a routine matter. If the child falls ill, peace is totally gone. Even changing the nappies, putting the child to sleep or playing and talking to the non verbal child needs professional training altogether.

Parents don't want their children to suffer all those situations that they had experienced in their times. The burning desire of growing teenagers for independence can lead to conflict between parent and child. The younger generation is full of enthusiasm but lacks maturity. Even many parents are not trained to deal with the growing problems of adolescence.

Finally, families must learn to cope with ageing parents and grandparents. When every body is healthy, life seems to be comfortable. But old age itself is a disease. There are many routine problems attached to old age. The old can sometimes behave in a childishly immature way which is difficult to accept because in the past he has been proved to be very mature, intelligent and balanced. One is normally not prepared to live with this kind of atmosphere.

Social Need

This involves interaction with other people. Getting your work done, asking a person for an appointment, pressure for public speaking, sudden outbursts of anger or compulsion to extend care are common stress factors. Attending parties may be a source of enjoyment for one person but may be stressful for the person who likes quiet evenings at home. On the other hand, the outgoing person may find staying at home very stressful.

Even the strong feeling to maintain a dignified social status itself can lead to stress. From self identification as the topper in one community, we get ourselves also identified as belonging to a particular community in our society. For getting acceptance at a wider level there is an inner need for recognition, say as the favourite leader of the group. Still, many people feel isolated and chronically strive to find a feeling of social support. Social stress factors vary widely from person to person. What brings relief to one person from one stress may contribute to the stress of another person.

Fear Of Change

Every person has his own limits of absorbing change. In this century the rate of change has been accelerating at a speed previously unimaginable. As most people are not attuned to the concept of change, they find difficulty in accepting change. Change for good or bad, both are equally disturbing. Imagine any person getting a sudden jump in his career. From the position of a manager in one department, he gets an opportunity to become the company's Managing Director. As he is not developed to adjust to that position, he feels disturbed and, really not happy.

We experience stress when anything important in life is changed. When we leave a job, a house or a relationship, part of our adjustment to our loss or to our new situation involves stress. When we move from one part of the country or city to another, we experience the change of uprooting. Loss of our social network and supports can be very stressful.

FEAR OF CHANGE

Chemical Reactions

Chemical stressors may include any drug a person abuses, such as alcohol. Chemical stressors also include the pesticides or sweeteners in foods we eat. Caffeine is a common chemical stressor. Nicotine in tobacco is another. Most drugs, both those that are sold under prescription and those that are sold over the counter are chemical stressors.

We freely choose to ingest most chemical stressors. At the same time some chemical stressors are less under our control. For example, we may live in a city where we drink chemicals in the water. Likewise, many foods, particularly processed ones, have chemical additives. We may ingest large quantities of alcohol or smoke. Even non-smokers also can't escape smoke. In parties as also in offices smokers are contributing silently towards the harmful effects of smoking.

Work Pressures

Work stressors are tensions and pressures we usually experience between nine and five o'clock at our place of work. If you are a homemaker, your hours may be longer. Asking the boss for a raise, trying to meet impossible deadlines, working late hours, explaining an embarrassing mistake, disciplining your children, or cleaning the floor a second time to remove fresh mud tracks are all work stressors. Whereever we live and whatever work we do, if not properly understood and managed, will lead to work pressures.

Work stressors, like social stressors, differ from person to person. One person may work well under pressure of deadlines and find slow periods boring and stressful. Another person may get uptight and stressed when given a deadline.

Some jobs generally involve more work stressors than others. Did you know that secretaries suffer more from stress than executives do, as measured by the incidence of such stress-related problems as heart disease, high blood pressure, ulcers and nervous disorders? We believe the changing nature of our working world is a major contributor to stress. Even long back people didn't know everyone on their staff by first name. And now businesses have mushroomed and, frequently, have hierarchies of managers. Most of us have little personal contact with our "real" boss with whom we may find it frustrating even to meet or communicate our needs. The "home office" or the "corporation" often acquire identities of their own; but how do you discuss your needs with the "home office" or the "corporation"?

Nowadays the sexual composition of the work force is also changing. Nearly 50 per cent of workforce now consists of women. This group includes half of all the mothers with school-age children. Economists predict that over the next ten years, the number of working women will increase and six women will enter the work force for every five men. Working women do not have only the responsibility of their job, but they also have household commitments. Family members keep on expecting care and attention from them as a result of which they are under great pressure.

Other changes have also occurred in the working world. Fifty per cent of the working force is white-collar. Fewer jobs are linked to end products such as merchandise or food. It has become more and more difficult to see the value of our individual contributions.

The importance of work stress in predicting life span was demonstrated in a government task force study on longevity and the work force. The study found that more than any measure of physical health such as the use of tobacco, or genetic inheritance, the number one factor in longevity in this country is work satisfaction.

Rational Decisions

It has become more and more difficult to make decisions both on and off the job. Rational decisions depend on our ability to predict the consequences of our actions. Now our ability to make the best predictions is often compromised by more alternatives and less decision time. A good example of vocational decision stress is reflected in the occupational alternatives available to us.

Now the number of choices we have is overwhelming. A brief look at the thousands of jobs available confirms the potential for confusion. Decision stress on the job is also increasing. Certain jobs, these days, carry too much responsibility with too little authority. People normally experience ambiguity and conflicting job demands. Predictability and control in our rapidly changing world culture are increasingly unattainable. There are more possibilities to consider, but humans have only a limited capacity to receive, process and then retain information. If you plan to push beyond certain limits, your stress response may sound an alarm.

As part of human nature, people feel very comfortable to identify themselves with what so ever they come across. They get identified with the parents, spouse, children, relations, a particular house, company, city, state, country, continent and even the world. They also get themselves identified with their job, business, car, computer and even the smallest possible things like pen and hairstyle, etc.

When a person gets promotion normally he feels very happy. But, at the same time, he is confused and highly uncomfortable. He gets so much identified with his previous designation and responsibility that even after the two years of his promotion he still retains his old identity. When people change their house or even the job, they feel highly disturbed because they have been too much identified with the people around. The main problem is how to cope in an unfamiliar environment.

In a life time people normally take a maximum of ten steps, e.g., getting married, promotion or shifting a house, etc. Every step taken gives them a combination of confused pleasures and sufferings. Our life is not just ten steps. If full life is taken as hundred years, imagine the number of months, weeks, days, hours, minutes, seconds or even the moments we are really living. Are just ten steps sufficient? Are we only living our life for pleasures and sufferings and not for happiness?

Never Get Identified With Any Step In Life

Move Ahead Moment By Moment

Commuting Problems

Many people commute long distances to work. Some people drive in rush-hour traffic daily. Others spend hours on a bus or train while still others travel to the minimum. Depending on our distance from work, the amount of traffic we encounter and our mode of travel, commuting may or may not be a major stressor.

Phobia

Many people have exaggerated fears of certain animals, places, objects, or situations which they imagine pose an immediate danger. These intense and recurrent fears are called phobias. The range of phobias is unlimited and there are Greek names for almost anything a person can fear.

Some of the common objects of unreasonable fear include claustrophobia (a fear of being shut in a closed place), acrophobia (heights), hydrophobia (the fear of water) and in some children, school phobia. Social phobias can be specific fears of activities such as speaking in front of large groups or meeting new people.

One person was bitten by a dog at the age of six. For eighteen years, he was afraid of dogs - not just the dog that bit him but most dogs, chained or unchained! This is an example of a conditioned fear. Many of these people do not remember the connection or link that caused the phobia. Infact his fear exaggerated and he forgot how it started; but by carefully avoiding dogs, he had never learned to overcome his phobic anxiety.

He fell in love with a woman whom he wanted to marry. But there was a problem. She not only loved him but also dogs. She wanted to raise a beautiful dog when they could afford a home with a yard. This did not stop him from marrying the woman he loved because buying their own home seemed very far off in the future. As the days and years passed, he could feel the dogs through his wife's experiences. He could know the difference between a normal and mad dog. A normal dog will bite only out of his self defence. If you mean no harm to the dog, the dog has no reason to bite you. Over the period he was able to overcome his phobia. This is an example of how a stressor can become a source of pleasure and recreation.

Physical Work Load

Physical stressors are demands that change the state of our bodies. Physical stressors can be the strain we feel when we physically overextend ourselves, fail to get enough sleep or nutritious diet, or suffer an injury. Pregnancies and menstrual discomforts are examples of physical stressors that are specific to women.

Physical stressors that people normally experience often involve increased physical demands. Working seventy to eighty hours each week without getting adequate rest can place a heavy physical demand on the body. We don't feel stress only during work as is commonly believed. An abrupt change from high pressured, sustained activity to the boredom of low activity can also be a stressor. For example, some heart attacks occur immediately after a busy period of time when a person finally retires from his hectic job.

Onset of Disease

Disease, be it short term or long term is an important stress factor. Many disease stress factors are short term and place us under immediate but time-limited stress. No doubt we remain uncomfortable for a short while but recover within a couple of days.

Let us concentrate here on some of the chronic diseases that last a life time particularly those that may have been inherited. Some people are born with a predisposition to develop chronic headaches, high blood pressure, arthritis, asthma, allergies, ulcers, diabetes, dermatitis, hyperthyroidism or multiple sclerosis, etc.

Stress has its direct or indirect effect on practically each and every system of the body. The above mentioned conditions may or may not be visibly caused by stress. Nonetheless, they can be aggravated by stress. With the onset of stress, every disease may increase in intensity. The attacks of the disease may last longer and the frequency of the episodes may increase. Accordingly, with effective and timely management of stress, the recovery can be equally fast and acceptable.

It is an unchallenged theory that genetically each person has one or more weak systems within his or her body. For example, if one or both of the parents of a young man may have diabetes, he should monitor his blood sugar more frequently than a person without a known family history of diabetes. Knowledge of our weak system could enable us to use our body as a barometer of stress.

Maintain Health By Knowing Your Weak System

Experiencing Pain

New and old injuries, accidents, or diseases give us aches and pains. Pains that cause people stress over a long period of time are particularly important. Old traumas to the joints, for example, can leave a person with a painful osteoarthritis. This condition, like a chronic disease, can flare up at times of stress. A person with headaches may be plagued by chronic pain. In periods of stress, the pain may become more severe, last longer and occur more frequently. The stress of any chronic pain may result in a reduction of both physical and social activities. Thus, the stress of chronic pain may lead to still more stress through isolation and inactivity. Ultimately, it may lead to depression.

Environmental Situations

Our surroundings that are often unavoidable, such as noisy typewriters, cramped offices, smoke-filled rooms, choking exhaust fumes and the burning heat of summer or the chilling cold of winter, are our environmental stress factors. Extreme environmental stimuli or conditions, both excessive and scanty, almost always cause stress. Loud noise is stressful, but studies in special sound-insulated rooms have also demonstrated that total silence can also be highly stressful.

Purpose

To initiate the path of understanding as to how to manage stress in your life.

What To Do

Identify ten stress factors in your life. Now plan how would you manage these one by one.

Purpose

To develop an understanding whether you really want to manage stress in your life or not.

What To Do

Make a list of ten situations where you are too much under stress. Workout a plan on how to come out of these.

___

___

___

___

___

___

___

___

___

___

___

___

___

___

___

___

___

Purpose

To know your weak system for maintaining your health.

What To Do

Identify ten physical weaknesses within yourself and lay out plans to come out of those.

CHAPTER 4

DO WE REALLY HAVE A CHOICE?

STRESS

PROBLEMS

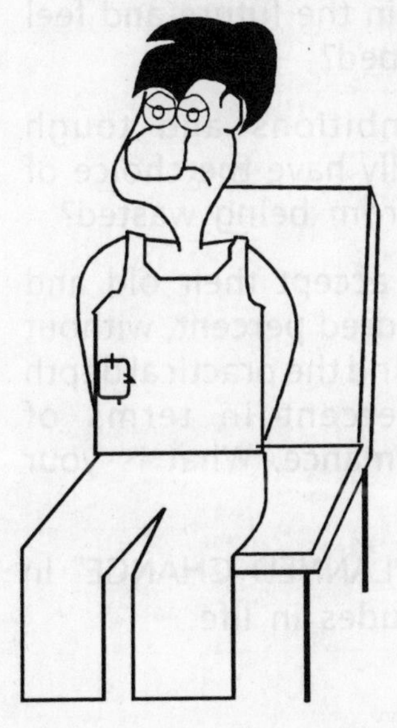

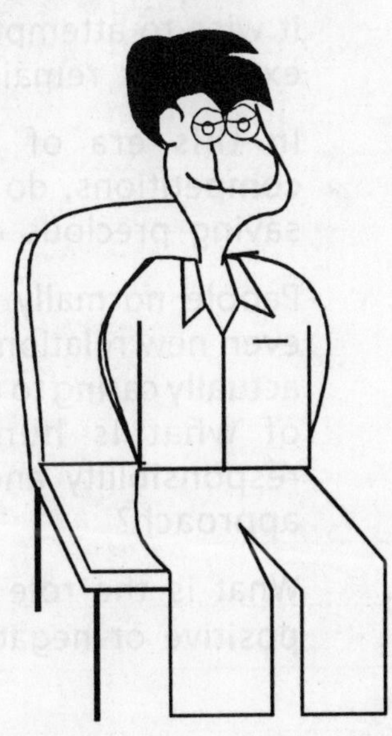

NO ESCAPE   NO PROBLEM

Explore Yourself

1. You don't want to miss a very important appointment. You are waiting to board a train but the train is late. What will you do?

2. It is felt that for a person on the path of achievement, a degree of stress is necessary to rouse his motivation and maintain his commitment towards his performance. Give your opinion.

3. In your opinion what is the role of fantasy and reality in practical life situations?

4. When you know that the future is unknown, is it wise to attempt to live in the future and feel excited or remain disturbed?

5. In this era of high ambitions and tough competitions, do you really have the choice of saving precious energy from being wasted?

6. People normally tend to accept their old and even new relations in hundred percent, without actually caring to understand the practical depth of what is hundred percent in terms of responsibility and performance. What is your approach?

7. What is the role of "UNPLANNED CHANGE" in positive or negative attitudes in life.

Learning Objectives

By the end of this chapter, you will be able to:

- ❖ Understand the role of fantasy and reality in practical life situations.
- ❖ Learn to accept and live in the present.
- ❖ Accept others according to your capacity rather than their total needs.
- ❖ Have clarity that change is life and life needs change, so plan the choice accordingly.

We are already aware that life is full of situations. An escape from one tough situation would lead to many more troublesome situations, which seem harder to face and difficult to escape from. In such a life surrounded by varied situations, do we really have a choice?

What choice does a person have if her fiancee meets with an accident? If her only child gets three red marks despite heavy expenses on tuition. Her sister-in-law comes for dinner with her family unexpectedly when she is running high fever and the servant is on leave. Inspite of her best efforts her subordinate becomes her boss. Half of the staff suddenly goes on leave when there is an urgent assignment to be completed. Does the person really have a choice?

Obviously we can't escape. The only choice is to accept and deal with the prevailing situation. May be we don't have the expertise today, which means we have room for development. The need thus is to learn the art of managing tough, and not so tough, situations.

These unmanageable situations come to us in the form of stress, which is an integral part of our life. It is both externally and internally generated. External stress is experienced usually by a change of job, house, relations or any similar event. Change always takes us away from the level of previous identification. Because we don't feel prepared to accept the change for our betterment, we become bitter in our feelings and behaviour.

Internal stress is caused by the conflict between our real and fantasy worlds. It is human nature to go beyond the present. Whether it is a positive (say a thrilling) or negative (say a shocking) experience we tend to feel uncomfortable. We find difficulty in establishing a logical link with our present self. In imagination we experience something different, which does not match what we have with us in reality. If we enjoy anything only in our imagination and leave it there, then there is no harm.

The word 'stress' normally means any stimulus that may harm the body. ONLY UNMANAGEABLE SITUATIONS RESULTING IN STRESS LEAD TO THE ILL AND UNACCEPTABLE EFFECTS.

Stress that is well managed is indeed an opportunity to grow in life. That way every moment of life becomes peaceful, fresh, and happy.

Path of Development

It is felt that for a person on the path of achievement a degree of stress is necessary to arouse his motivation and maintain his commitment towards his performance. Because his goals may not be very clearly defined, he needs a constant stimulus to perform. Too little stimulus results in a sense of flatness, which can lead to inertia or apathy. The accountability system planned and implemented by his boss can be the best stimulus.

Not only can the optimum amount of stress help to raise the level of performance, but it can also be enjoyable and exhilarating too. A challenging job, for example, is a stimulus in itself, and its successful completion resolves the stress factor. It becomes a point of celebration and gives lots of freshness and energy.

There is a thin line between a healthy and an unhealthy stimulus. It's only when pressure goes beyond a healthy limit that problems arise. In a state of challenge, we are normally never prepared for the negative to happen. We feel acutely shocked by a failure, which was never expected in the first place. It becomes very difficult to come out of that shaky situation. Here we require some constructive support to recover.

Acceptance Level

As a rule, it's impossible to determine the optimum amount of stress, people, in general, can bear. Even the death of a loved one will produce very different degrees of response from different people. One may feel totally shattered, another may recover with the support of friends and relations to restart his life, while still another may accept that painful fact and return immediately to his present responsibilities.

It's important to get to know our own acceptance level. That may sound easy but in practice it can be difficult. How can we know our acceptance level without actually undergoing that negative experience? The typical negative experience will help us feel the depth to accept.

The relationship between any stress factor and us is a highly complex one, governed by all kinds of variables, including individual attitudes and beliefs. It is directly based on the depth we have gained through our past experience.

But the way we decide to cope with stress depends to a great extent on beliefs and attitudes, and we are to avoid serious damage to our health. Luckily our attitudes and beliefs also keep on changing with the passage of life.

It is of course difficult to evaluate our own attitudes and beliefs honestly and objectively. But there is no choice. Here the power of our imagination comes into play. Without practically losing anything or anybody, we can very well feel the depth of possible loss in our imagination only. This will help us know and develop our acceptance level. The moment we learn to accept the situation around us, life falls within manageable limits.

Fantasy vs Reality

Mr. Fantastic was working as a marketing executive in a multinational company. He had always been dreaming of becoming a rich and influential person one-day. He had dreamt of his future status, that of a man with power, the luxury of an air-conditioned car, a sophisticated life style, and a charming wife. To justify the future position in reality he would always practice the same mannerisms like wearing the costliest clothes bought from the most expensive showrooms, treating friends to dinner only at five star restaurants.

Needless to say he generally used to run out of money before the middle of the month. He could barely satisfy his job responsibilities and home commitments. Often he had to change his jobs; this never allowed him to pursue a stable and dignified career.

Many a time, like Mr. Fantastic, we don't accept reality; but, fantasy is not available for any practical living purpose. If there's a close degree of harmony between the world as it is and the world as it is desired to be, stress is absent. Many a time, it happens like this: we didn't have time to plan the future but what came in for us was comfortable. It may also happen that whatsoever we planned almost came about. However, it may not always happen.

If reality and our fantasy differ widely, stress is present and, varied reactions like depression and stubbornness are possible. Depending on our level of non-acceptance there may be mild to severe irritation.

While planning our goal perhaps, we did not consider the present resources and situation. We also didn't consider the possible obstacles we might face during performance.

To take an example, we are waiting for a train and the train is late. Our reaction is that it shouldn't be. Reality as it's perceived is that the train is late. Reality as fantasized is that train should always be on time; so, our irritation results from the failure of reality to match our expectation. If nothing can be done and the delay means that we will miss an important appointment, the level of stress may be extremely high.

Lack of opportunity for releasing these pent up emotions produces harmful consequences. If, however, we telephone the person concerned and explain why we will be late, the stress will be reduced. If we can – and do – take another form of transport, and thus avoid being late altogether, although we may remain annoyed in the process; the stress would have disappeared.

Living in the Present

Feeling of uncertainty about the future is a common source of stress. Who knows the future? Even leading astrologers can only speculate about various possibilities but they can never be sure. Had they known their future and also had control over it, they would have been the happiest persons in the world. But it is not so. Even the astrologers are by and large disturbed in their respective lives.

The future is unknown; therefore, whatever we tend to fantasize is felt as reality in our own minds. Because all fantasies take off from the present, we feel like accepting fantasy as an extension of reality only. We have the liberty to generate enormous degrees of stress, worrying about those events which, in fact, may never happen.

Ms. Fantastic wanted to marry a handsome milieu sophisticated executive from the multinational. But her parents fixed her match with a graduate Mr. Entrepreneur who was short statured and running his own motor parts business. Mr. Entrepreneur is a reality and the fantasy person is a myth.

For the first five years of her marriage she kept on brooding over her fate and blaming her parents. Life had turned into hell. She decided to go in for a divorce. Her advocate helped her assess and understand the present circumstances. He also enabled her to feel dignified and there seemed no opportunity of getting married to her fantasy person.

Once she accepted her present husband, she found him to be an extremely understanding and caring person. She learnt to accept his physical appearance and felt proud to stand by his side. And they lived happily ever after. The key to avoid the harmful effects lies in recognizing whether or not we can do anything to resolve the conflict between reality and fantasy. If we can, we should do it; otherwise, we should reconcile ourselves to our present reality. The fact is we have no choice: reality must be accepted.

Mr. X had misplaced an important file in the office. The boss was about to come to discuss some relevant information from that file. What was to be done? He tried his best to locate that file but all in vain. "What will the boss think about me? He will treat me as a totally irresponsible person. He can even sack me. How will I find a new job? What would happen to my image in society, my wife's treatment, my children, their school fees .....". His mind was a whirl.

To Avoid
Harmful Effects
Of Stress

If You Can
Do Anything
Then Do It

If Not
Accept Reality

The boss hadn't come as yet. But the mind had already gone astray. It was filled with negative thoughts: he was under uncalled for stress. The boss came and happened to have the file in his brief case. Because of the habit of going into the future without assessing the facts, he couldn't even remember that only yesterday the boss had taken that file from him to study it.

Part of the solution to this lies in learning to live in the present and not attempting to live in the future. We must pay due regard to practical preparation for future events and, at the same time, not allow our imagination to start drifting towards what if such and such happens.......... When such and such actually happens, it can be looked into at that time. There is every possibility that it may not happen at all. It is no use targeting your arrows at blind goals. Concentrate your attention only on the present. It is easy and practical.

At times, stress is due to some unknown fear. When the past starts interfering with the present, there is a fear that the same will happen in future too. No two situations are exactly alike, so, comparison is irrelevant. There is a lot of difference between trying to have faith and achieving total faith. There is no mental peace when one is just attempting to perform while going through many ups and downs, to do or not to do, and the mind is never at rest; so, a lot of energy is wasted in just trying to convince one's own self.

One must learn to have faith in oneself, only then would it be possible to have faith in others. By accepting and living in the present, that faith in oneself and others is automatically and logically established.

A Matter of Choice

Everyone has the ability to reach to external stresses in a variety of ways. There are always many possibilities to manage our stresses. But somehow most people ignore the choices available to them. The very first idea coming to their mind seems to be the only possible solution, which many a time is either not viable or not possible at all. When we are not aware of the various choices available to us, we practically feel helpless. We receive what is not meant for us and our precious energy is just wasted. Do we have the choice to save our precious energy from being wasted?

A response is always the result of choice, even though it might appear to be otherwise. The fact is that when nothing has actually happened we have the choice to go negative or positive in our imagination. We can choose to feel angry, jealous, guilty, bitter, irritated and so on. Many people, out of ignorance, tend to go negative only, as if the positive will never happen. We can also choose to be happy, giving, forgiving, loving, and accepting.

We must learn to accept what can't be altered and to tackle constructively what can be. Many a time people take their misunderstanding as their understanding and thus, remain confused and disturbed. They feel they are on the right track while the fact is – they are not. Because they are operating from the wrong base, their every visible move towards understanding will only lead to unwanted misunderstanding. This way the clouds of confusion enveloping their minds will keep on multiplying towards unknown destinations.

A MATTER OF CHOICE

Relationships

Personal relationships are full of problems, anxiety and stress pitfalls. We normally decide to accept our relations in hundred percent without actually caring to understand the depth of what is hundred percent in terms of responsibility and performance. When the other person starts behaving with the base of offered hundred percent depth we feel uncomfortable. It is important to accept others according to our capacity rather than their needs till hundred percent depth in the relation has been felt and established.

Misunderstandings, expectations, feelings of inadequacy or being taken for granted etc. generate emotional pressures. We have no choice is selecting our blood relations but we definitely have a choice in selecting our friends. That means friendly relations are supposed to be the best. Then, why do we find friends turning into enemies? It happens only when we accept our contacts as friends without establishing mutual faith and understanding.

"The other person has accepted me and now will do everything for me," is the initial feeling of many people in the very first helpful dealing. We keep on expecting from others under the dignified cover of self-imagined acceptance. The other person may also have needs and feel uncomfortable because his needs are not being met. Then, why should he accept us and be prepared with total commitment to care. Acceptance and commitment have to be reciprocated.

It is easy to enter into a relationship, but it needs careful nurturing to see it through various storms of life, and that too, for a lifetime. Before making any commitment one must understand the meaning of commitment very clearly along with the associated responsibilities.

However, the important thing is to deal with others, as you want to be dealt with. Before dealing with the other person, let us just imagine the same thing being done to us by that person. How do we feel in that situation? Highly uncomfortable or comfortable? If it is even just uncomfortable, stop and plan again so that the other person feels comfortable. This way, automatically, he will develop total commitment towards us.

Accepting Change

Even the situations that bring about change are the source of most external stress factors. Stress can be very easily caused by so many external sources. Apart from the routine sources, these include, excessive noise, excessive heat or cold, repetitive activities, and such bad experiences as commuting on an unreliable transport system, or having to drive in heavy traffic for hours every day.

Extreme external stress factors are often endured by people in potentially dangerous jobs. If we are in such a job, it becomes very important for us to learn to remain calm and composed.

It is possible only if our mind accepts the possible dangers of the job itself and then plan various remedial measures. If any remedial measure is not visibly possible, we must accept that loss as a part of our balance sheet of happiness. The resultant profitability in the balance sheet will indeed give us the happiness.

Differences in individual personalities and behaviour must be borne in mind when assessing a person on the effects of stress. A highly stressful change indicates a high probability of health being affected. The key word here is 'probability'.

Depending on somebody's background the reactions are variably different. A person brought up in tough environment will feel comfortable even in the world's toughest of situations. While a pampered person from the very childhood will be under heavy pressure even for the minor events of life.

Thus it cannot be overemphasized how differently people react when exposed to stress. In some rare cases heavy pressures have been shown to have non apparent effect on health. In fact, when we accept the onset of heavy pressures, our mind is immediately freed from negativity, the attitude at that time being constructive and positive.

Remember, it's not just one situation but continual stress that leads to problems; so, if it's feasible we must space changes in our lives as much as we can. Often, however, we don't have any control over events; so, the objective is to adapt our responses to them. If we can't manage the stress in the present then plan some source of entertainment in between stress situations. Our main focus is on minimizing the effects of stress and avoiding stress-induced ill health.

For example, a professor will take to gardening for a change, while a gardener will take to reading books for a change. What we do is not very important, but any activity of a different nature is a must for a change and provides relief. Let us remember.......

Change
Is Life
And
Life
Needs
Change

Minimizing The Load

Because stress is cumulative, a relatively minor event, when added to a large existing stress load, will often prove to be more than what the body's adaptation processes can cope with. It is equally important to keep on disposing off the stresses we are facing, one by one. Otherwise, there will be an overlapping of our stresses.

The load can be easily decreased if we relegate our stresses to competent subordinates who can handle those situations.

The smooth functioning of these processes can all too easily be undermined by the abuse of various aspects of daily life. Everyone can, in fact, control personal habits and life-styles, the amount or quality of exercise, nutrition, rest, sleep and relaxation.

Drinking Stress

A wise man said, "Don't eat but drink your food". The idea is that if we chew it to the level when it becomes liquid then digestion becomes easy. Food well digested will lead to good health. Similarly, we must drink out stress to the level of its digestion. Any life situation, if not properly understood, will lead to stress.

For a skilled heart surgeon performing open heart surgery is very easy, while for a physician even stitching a simple wound may look like an impossible task. The idea is to thoroughly understand all the aspects of the stress situation so that it does not remain stressful and becomes easy to handle.

Drinking Stress

Sleep

The value of rest and sleep cannot be over estimated. Sleep is an integral part of life. Nobody can keep on working and working throughout life. Why to talk of life, people do not feel comfortable if they are required to work nonstop even for twenty-four hours.

Rest means total non-performance at the body and mind level. To get excellent results we must learn the art of balancing performance and nonperformance. Anybody who decides to perform, and only perform, will end up in failure, and ultimately frustration.

It's worth emphasizing here that stress can result in a disturbance of the regular sleep pattern and lead to insomnia. Insomnia or the inability to sleep leads to debility of both, the body and the mind. A battery charger will recharge the cells or the batteries. Similarly, sleep also recharges our body and mind to the level of full vigour and vitality. We feel refreshed to perform anything difficult after a good night's sleep.

The converse is also true. Sleep disturbances create stress and promote depression. It is a complex chain reaction. If a totally relaxed and happy-go-lucky person, for any reason, gets a sleepless night then, the next morning he does not feel fresh and energetic.

As a result he will not be producing quality results in his job. What will be the result? Because of the non-acceptance of his poor quality results he will face stress from his working environment and in turn, it will automatically lead to more sleep disturbances.

Muscle Lethargy and Spasm

This may result from emotional stress. Whenever we are worrying, it snatches away our energy which is equally required for our muscles. We feel drained out, resulting in lethargy and spasm of our muscles. But it may also be caused by lack of exercise, poor posture or habitual working positions such as hunching over a desk all day. Our muscles also work on the principle of demand and supply. No doubt the food we take gives us a lot of energy but if there is no demand for energy in the body, all of the generated energy goes waste. When muscles perform, the demand for energy is created in the body and the supply is accordingly utilized.

Lack of muscular exercise results in a situation of no demand; and emotional stress drains out the presently available energy. This way out our system is unduly disturbed. Such muscular disturbances feed backward impulses via the nervous system and deactivate the central nervous system so that mental relaxation is also prevented.

In other words, just as a mental state can create physical discomfort, a prolonged degree of muscular spasm and lethargy can influence the emotional or mental state. It is also a chain reaction. It is within our control to make it a positive or negative chain.

Physical exercise, as well as relaxation techniques and manipulation of the soft tissues or deep massage, can give freshness and energy to muscles. Our personal habits are responsible for the health of our body and mind. So we must ....

Control Personal Habits And Life-styles

Nutrition

Unbalanced nutrition is the all too often root cause of a general feeling of being below par and can lower the body's resistance to stress. Despite this, in the developed and the developing world, the principles of a balanced diet are often ignored. For example, sugar consumption has shot up over the past 100 years or so; not only does sugar provide a lot of calories without any nutrients, but the over-consumption of foods containing highly refined sugar can lead to hyperglycaemia (high blood sugar) in borderline cases.

Sometimes, because of intake of antidiabetic drugs there can be a visible fluctuation of blood sugar levels in the body which produces wild swings in mood and behaviour. If our blood sugar is low, our reaction to external stress factor will remain highly unpredictable.

Low intake of fresh and unprocessed foods, especially vegetables, fruits, pulses, whole grains and nuts can result in vitamin deficiency, in which a string of interrelated vitamins, minerals, and enzymes is lacking. This creates an internal environment that prevents the body from countering stress adequately. By taking care of these aspects of our daily life, which are the easiest to alter, we'll be going a long way towards equipping ourselves to counter stress.

Purpose

To develop the ability to accept and live in the present.

What To Do

Make a list of ten situations of the past where you had faced problems because of non-acceptance of present and attempting to live in the future. Feel how you can re-live the same situations peacefully.

Purpose

How to accept others according to your capacity rather than their total needs.

What to Do

Identify ten situations where while helping others, you had experienced problems for yourself. If you were to live the same situation again what would be your strategy?

CHAPTER 5

REDUCING TENSION TIME

Explore Yourself

1. Whenever you have some physical problem everybody around you cares for you but when you have some problem in the mind, perhaps nobody cares. Why?

2. People normally tell you not to worry but perhaps nobody tells how not to worry. What should you do?

3. A room is full of smoke which is gradually increasing. You want to get rid of the suffocating smoke. What should be your strategy?

4. Many people, in a mood to manage tension and strain, end up feeling frustrated. Why?

5. One must be carefree but responsible too. Many people claim to be carefree but the fact is they behave carelessly. Give your opinion.

6. How far is it possible for you to avoid stress?

7. How do you feel when you are compelled to look after an unwanted guest?

8. In perfection you feel happy only at the end and that too if you have achieved as per the set standards, while in excellence you are automatically geared up to gain success and happiness every moment. Do you still want to attain perfection?

Learning Objectives

By the end of this chapter, you will be able to :

- ❖ plan for yourself on how to escape from worry.
- ❖ identify that in problem situations releasing tension is no permanent solution.
- ❖ know how to reduce tension time.
- ❖ understand the practical difference between aiming at perfection and striving for excellence.
- ❖ convert a complaint into a problem.

Tension is a silent killer. This statement appears to be a little difficult to digest. When a person is physically sick, all members of his family are disturbed. The spouse remains awake throughout the night, the son goes to each and every place to get the medicines, all the relatives keep on enquiring about his health, or even make courtesy visits. Everybody understands his physical condition and extends full care accordingly.

But when one has any problem in the mind, normally, nobody seems to be concerned. People tend to ignore it completely. There is a general feeling that it is all psychological. As if a psychological problem is no problem at all. Even when one goes to the family physician, he tells the relatives not to worry because it is all psychological or, in medical language, he says it is functional. Surprisingly, the people who claim to love the person, automatically start feeling and behaving in a carefree manner. Perhaps they are right. The doctor has confirmed him to be a normal person physically and even mentally. He has no pathological abnormality. The person is confused why the people, who normally care, are not caring now. Even the relatives are confused; if he has been declared normal why doesn't he behave normally. There is a feeling of an increasing distance.

Lack Of Understanding

There is no focus on understanding the ailing person. It is a simple fact that the word problem is attached to the word 'psychological'. Every problem definitely has a solution. Of course, it needs a totally different kind of management, different from the management of any physical problem. The solution will only be initiated when we accept his condition as a problem.

Both the parties are confused and keep on blaming each other. When we are not aware of the solution, we normally prefer to admit that it is not our problem. It is an easy escape. When we don't own the problem how can we own the linked responsibility? But, by claiming not to own the problem, do we mean to say that it does not belong to us? Whom are we befooling? Is it wise to befool oneself? In fact, by not owning, we are simply delaying the solution. Delay always complicates confusing situations. The visible circumstances have changed further. What we had planned earlier has become totally invalid. It now needs a new level of assessment. Decision to avoid the problem for the time being is different from ignoring it. Once ignored, we completely lose track and control of that problematic situation and it becomes more and more complicated.

As we know escape is simply not possible. We can't afford to ignore the problem situation. We have limited resources. The delay will further reduce them. When resources are diminishing, the present uncomfortable situation looks more magnified. In fact, it increases in its intensity.

With lack of understanding, the focus has entirely been shifted from the person and his problem. They behave like invisible enemies. No doubt love in the relationship still exists but care has disappeared. Any intention to care does not match the performance to care. Why and how should anybody care? There is no visible problem. As per their understanding the person is absolutely normal. Physically fit, yes. But mentally he is highly disturbed. Who has the competence to judge? At the most, the feeling is, "He has gone mad." The only possible care they can even dream of is sympathy. The poor chap! He was a dynamic person earlier. Maybe God is not kind to him.

Under these circumstances the relatives tend to disown him and his problem; thus, they own no responsibility towards the solution. A simple approach is to attack. "All your investigations are within normal range. Why don't you stop worrying, even the doctor has said so", is the normal statement. They want to look intelligent and great. The person is highly confused. His stress is further building up. Earlier, he had the problem not very clear to him and now he has got one more problem: he has also developed the established disease of worrying. Everybody only says "Don't Worry" But.....

Nobody Tells How Not To Worry

The tragedy is that people, by and large, don't know "How Not To Worry". It is as if, as long as they are alive, the worries are to be lived with. Similarly, if a subordinate or the life partner is not compatible at the desired level of understanding, the result is – both have to accept to live in hell.

There is rarely a focus on understanding, accepting, and developing the self and the other person towards a happy and peaceful life. Is tension a must to be lived along? Is there no way out? Because almost everybody in this world is living a life full of tension, so we also must adopt the same style! Is it a compulsory courtesy? If we plan to live a happy and peaceful life, others might feel hurt because we are not following their footsteps!

Tension – No Direct Existence

Tension which is a silent killer has no independent existence of its own. It is linked with stress. Only stress creates tension. If there is no stress, or if it has already been effectively managed, then tension is simply not possible. How can we manage " that something " which does not have its own independent existence? To manage the quality of any fruit, nothing can be done with the fruit itself. Specific mixed breeding is planned for the seed.

Many people as per the depth of their knowledge plan to manage tension and strain. Unknowingly they only attempt to manage the impossible. If a person is asked to increase his height by two inches within the next five minutes it is not possible. If one still keeps on trying, he will get no results. Of course he can wear a heel of two inches but that is not what was meant. Similarly, in the attempt to manage tension they work very hard because they have been educated and trained on the concept that a life full of tension is no life. As per their understanding tension has to be managed. But, while managing tension, they end up feeling confused and frustrated. Inspite of their best efforts, happiness is far from being achieved. In fact the more efforts they put in, the more frustrated they feel.

At the most tension can be easily released through various techniques of relaxation. Some people take alcohol, play some game, or go to some dance party while others prefer to go to a temple for offering prayers and still others, even without understanding the true meaning and depth, follow various widely preached methods of meditation.

No doubt all methods of relaxation give temporary relief. But do we need a temporary solution? Perhaps not. Then what to do? Is there no importance of relaxation? Should we ignore relaxation altogether? Relaxation can, at the most, release tension but the stress remains.

A room is full of smoke which is gradually increasing. We want to get rid of this suffocating smoke. One method some people may adopt is to open all doors and windows. Will it serve the purpose? Can we have a smokeless room? Yes, temporarily we do have a false feeling. But surprisingly the smoke keeps on increasing in intensity. Quite alarming. Isn't it? What to do?

One method is to start worrying, remain tense and blame luck or any body else. The other approach is very simple. Focus must be on identifying the cause and dealing with it. Wherever smoke is visible, fire must be around. Focus on identifying the location of fire and extinguish it; now the smoke will automatically disappear through the windows: a good doctor doesn't manage the symptoms but the cause.

In real life, we keep on opening windows and rarely focus on the site of fire. We feel that by releasing tension, we are managing tension. Still we remain confused as to why the desired level of peace and happiness is not being achieved. Many people at this stage tend to go to astrologers to mend their stars. Astrology is a recognized and established forecasting technique. Forecasting is only meant for better understanding and acceptance of our future situations.

Many students don't study and still expect good results. Without studying how can one expect good performance in an examination? Can any amount of simple or highly complicated worship lead to good performance and results? Certainly not.

If we don't start the journey, how can we reach the destination. While planning a journey people keep this thing in mind. But in life they simply can't corelate the two. They just expect miracles. Perhaps they don't know that behind every miracle, there is a lot of planning and effort. People never focus on why a particular person is missing from gossip sessions but when his results become visible they are pleasantly shocked.

Releasing Tension Is No Permanent Solution

Once an infant, after the morning bath, was dressed up by his mother. Surprisingly, immediately after that he felt restless and started crying. She caressed him, even sung a lullaby but to no use. Her mother-in-law was also not at home. Restlessly she waited for more than two hours. Neither her mother-in-law came nor was the child comfortable. She took the child to the doctor who gave him some tranquillizers. Till the effect of the medicine the child kept on sleeping but again started crying. The other doctor gave him pain killers but to no purpose.

The child kept on crying and the mother was getting more and more confused. It appeared to her that there was no choice except to keep on changing the doctors. One week passed but the infant did not improve. She was even afraid of changing his clothes because the moment she touched him, he would start crying. Only under the influence of the medicine he had undisturbed sleep. Out of confusion and panic, she took the child to the Medical Institute. The doctor asked the mother to undress the child.

When she was taking off his clothes both the doctor and the mother were deeply shocked. One week ago while dressing up the child, the safety pin along the frock had pierced through the skin. How could the child be comfortable with the pin inside his skin? Can any number of medicines give him any permanent relief? Any method of relaxation can only be a temporary solution. Out of ignorance, many a time, the real cause is ignored. More delay in a permanent solution can make the situation more complicated.

The moment the pin was removed, the infant heaved a sigh of relief and his actual recovery started. Only at this stage the medicines were also effective as part of the healing process.

Releasing tension gives only a false feeling of a solution. The person is feeling confused because to the best of his understanding the maximum has been done. If that best has not worked at all, it means something must be wrong somewhere, but what could it be? That is not at all clear to him. The focus must be on stress and not on tension. As long as stress remains one can't feel relaxed and balanced; so, stress must be managed first.

Be Carefree But Responsible Too

One must be carefree but responsible too. Many people feel surprised " Carefree and responsible at the same time? How is it possible?". Though some people claim to be carefree, they are actually careless. Relaxation does not always mean that we will become carefree. Without managing stress, if you plan to relax yourself, you ultimately tend to develop a totally careless attitude towards your responsibilities.

When the daughter-in-law joins the family after marriage, the proud mother-in-law is initially very happy. Gradually, she is afraid to accept and face the new responsibility. Her, more than two decades old, authority is being silently challenged. There is a rising atmosphere of conflicts. She finds it difficult to understand her daughter-in-law and she also feels that her daughter-in-law does not understand her. There is an uncomfortable exchange of blames from both the sides.

As a dignified escape she devotes her time to religion. She declares, "Now I formally hand over all my responsibilities and the authority to my daughter-in-law." She forgets one crucial point that the daughter-in-law also needs training to accept and justify this new responsibility. She claims that she has become carefree but the fact is she has become careless.

Result Can Only Be Felt

Tension and Strain are the result of stress only. We can only feel the result but we can't manage it. Performance or the cause is in the present but the result will take us to the future. When we focus on the result it is an unrealized plan to live in the future. It is not possible to live in the future. When we attempt to do something which is impossible, we will only invite frustration as an unwanted guest.

Our wisdom tells us the difference between the possible and the impossible. Once we decide that something is impossible, we should not waste our precious energy in trying to do that. This is again a very simple concept and we know that the simple is always powerful. The fact remains that we don't want an uncomfortable result.

Whatever the result we can only feel that. So, the deeds must be planned and performed either with cause or performance. Stress creates tension and strain; so, our focus must be on managing stress only. We can't live a stress-free life but once the stress is managed we will live a life free from tension and strain, which indeed is the desired result.

When You Cannot Avoid Stress It Must Be Managed

Stress is an inevitable part of life. As we are in a continuous state of development, there will always be many situations which we can't manage with ease. It means that every unmanageable situation causes stress. We simply can't avoid it.

Delay Breeds Corruption

The need to tackle symptoms of stress is at the moment we feel them. " Delay breeds corruption "is a widely accepted dictum. The problematic situation at hand is surrounded by many irrelevant ideas. If an outsider is present during discussion of a delicate family situation, nobody in the group feels comfortable. That person may be very intelligent, even a proven consultant. But he is the odd person out in that group; thus, he becomes totally irrelevant. These irrelevant persons or ideas make us more and more unspecific in our approach. Automatically the solution gets delayed.

A simple way to manage situations is gradually moving on to a complex track. Because we have not trained ourselves in the art of managing irrelevant persons or ideas, we feel trapped in a situation. Inspite of our best efforts we are unable to live in peace and happiness. Delay means we are inviting unwanted complications. Inviting somebody as a guest means we are accepting the responsibility of looking after him properly. Our need is to manage and avoid that unwanted situation, but now we are feeling compelled to give our best of energy and resources by unwillingly living through it. We are feeling disturbed and can't blame anybody else for the same.

Managing a simple situation needs less energy while to deal with a complicated situation requires more energy. With a limited stock of energy, we are, gradually, becoming hollow from within. A lot of our energy has unnecessarily been wasted in undesirable destructive efforts. With less energy we can't even manage the next very simple situation.

The longer we ignore the stress situation, the harder it is to adjust to a state of relaxed well being. Infact we are straying from that desired state of comfort. Moreover, if we ignore it, then we are inviting anxiety. Every next moment is leading towards more and more discomfort. When we take a decision that we can't do anything, at least in that case, we won't be wasting our precious energy on an unacceptable track of performance.

Reducing Tension Time

Tension Time is that time during which we normally remain tense. Suppose our need is promotion. If we don't get the promotion for the next one year, we would remain tense for one year. If we get the promotion after one month, our tension time is reduced to one month. And if it comes after one week the tension time is reduced to one week. Similarly, if the promotion comes to you after one day, one hour, one minute or even one moment, the tension time is accordingly reduced. If we get a letter from the boss mentioning, "As per the company's new policy you will be promoted after one year", your tension disappears even though the promotion will come after one year. So ....

To Reduce Tension Time Develop The Habit Of Taking Correct And Quick Decisions

Should we just start practising to take correct and quick decisions without feeling the practical depth of how to take a decision? We have all read since our school days " Practice Makes Perfect ". Is it true? Perfection itself is a very confusing concept. Perfection normally means we have attained the ultimate. An Olympic champion is taken as perfect in his field. The person could become a champion only after more than a decade's devoted practice. But what happens the next time? Somebody else will come and break the record. Now, where is perfection?

Towards Excellence

Life is in a constant state of development. Whatever we accomplish today will leave more scope for further improvement. Perfection is possible only under very selective and specific conditions. Perfection can't be general. We need to set a specific target with well defined criteria. Achieving the same can be taken as one level of perfection. If we are keen to attain perfection as a working belief, we must keep on setting and achieving short term specific goals.

We must plan to move towards excellence. Perfection can be taken as a destination which also has a beginning. Attaining perfection is the end of a specific effort. Once a goal is achieved, there is the need to plan the next goal or there is an overlapping of many goals. It leads to a situation of fluctuating and jerky moments. For further growth we need to plan again and again. We live in an undefined fear of becoming blank again.

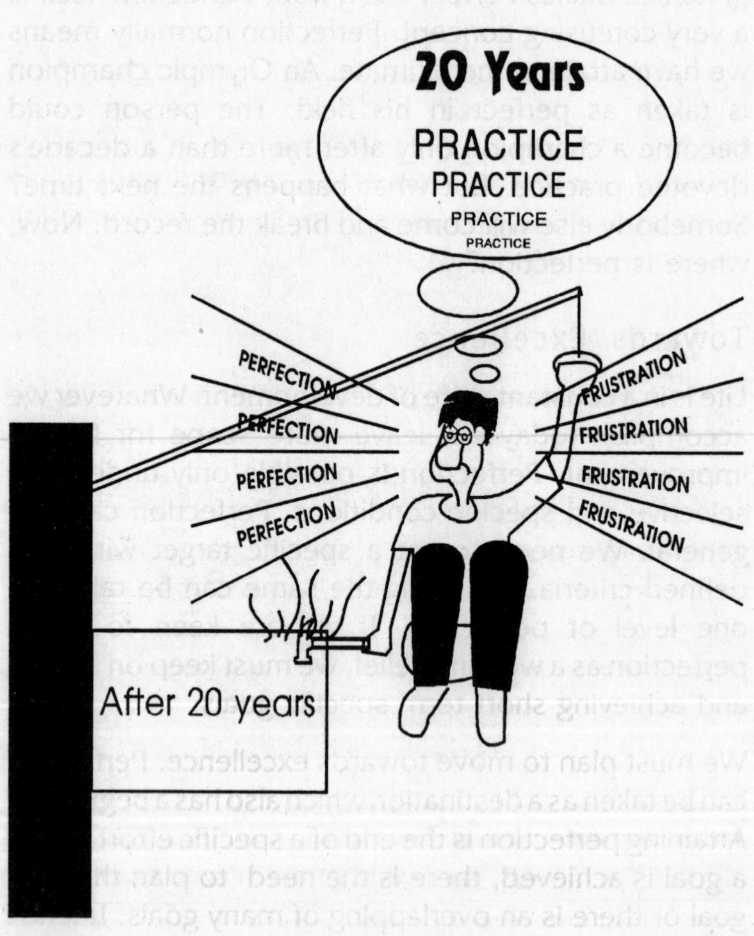
20 Years
PRACTICE
PRACTICE
PRACTICE
PRACTICE
PERFECTION
PERFECTION
PERFECTION
PERFECTION
FRUSTRATION
FRUSTRATION
FRUSTRATION
FRUSTRATION
After 20 years

While striving for excellence there is no visible end. It is a continuous journey. Staying on the path of excellence is smooth sailing. The mind is never blank. Because the track of performance is very clear, the mind remains very fresh and energetic. This way we are mentally prepared to grow every moment.

Normally, the word perfection is used in a positive sense. Excellence is always a positive term while perfection can also be sometimes negative, depending on the track we have chosen. In perfection we feel happy only at the end and that too if we have achieved as per the set standards. In excellence, we are automatically geared up to gain success and happiness every moment.

Practice May Not Make A Person Perfect

Practice is only a mechanical action and, by itself, lacks wisdom. Wisdom has a role to play only before we start practice. Sometimes, without a clear concept of what we wish to develop, we start practice. When we practice wrong methods in a wrong direction how can we attain the positive aspect of perfection? The unfelt reality is that we are straying away from positivity. At this stage if we realize the mistake, correcting it needs double the effort. First, we have to come back to the base level from where we started. And second, we have to restart towards the correct and the desired positive track. Imagine the amount of energy being wasted. It is important for us to realize the fact that......

Practice Generates Permanence Not Perfection

In fact, by practising on wrong lines, we will develop unacceptable habits. Habits once developed can't be changed overnight. The tragedy is that only people with whom we deal, make us realize that we have developed wrong habits. With our established unacceptable habits, they don't feel comfortable with uses. We wish people to love and come close to us, but we feel they are gradually deserting us. It is not very easy to accept such a situation.

Before we start practice, it becomes a must to develop a very clear concept of the correct method and the right direction. This way, on the desired track of positivity, we will gradually generate permanence. It becomes our responsibility not to allow tension to become a silent killer. Instead of trying to manage tension and ultimately developing a negative habit of attempting the impossible, we must first know that it is stress which creates tension. Our focus must be on stress.

Diagnosing a negative situation is the initial step towards Stress Management. When the diagnosis is correct the desired management by itself becomes very easy and within reach. But, if the problem itself has not been identified, no solution is possible. We must understand and follow simple powerful concepts.

Convert Complaint Into A Problem

People normally complain and say they have a problem. The complaint is non-specific. It is only a feeling, an attitude that doesn't have a solution. "I am feeling bored" is only a complaint for which no solution is possible. Being non-specific in nature, the complaint will only confuse the person and build up unnecessary stress.

Every complaint must be converted into a problem first. The problem is always specific, it can be observed, it can be measured. " I am feeling bored because I need a break from the routine or I don't have a VCR or I am not getting my salary or my car has run out of petrol", are some expressions of problems. These problems are specific in presentation and are equally specific in solution. In fact a solution is always hidden in the problem.

Once we have converted our complaint into a problem, we have automatically been diverted from the path leading to tension. It is the beginning of our journey towards peace and happiness.

Purpose

To feel that only the path of excellence will give you continuous peace and happiness.

What To Do

Recollect ten situations where you wanted to have perfection but experienced only frustration. Work out a plan of excellence for the same goals.

Purpose

To understand that reducing tension time is the simple key to peace and happiness.

What To Do

Identify ten situations from your past experience where you had felt a lot of tension. Now plan how you could have reduced your tension time.

Purpose

To learn to convert your complaining situations into specific problems.

What To Do

Make a list of ten complaining situations of your life. Now convert these into specific problems.

CHAPTER 6

UNDERSTANDING WORRY SITUATIONS

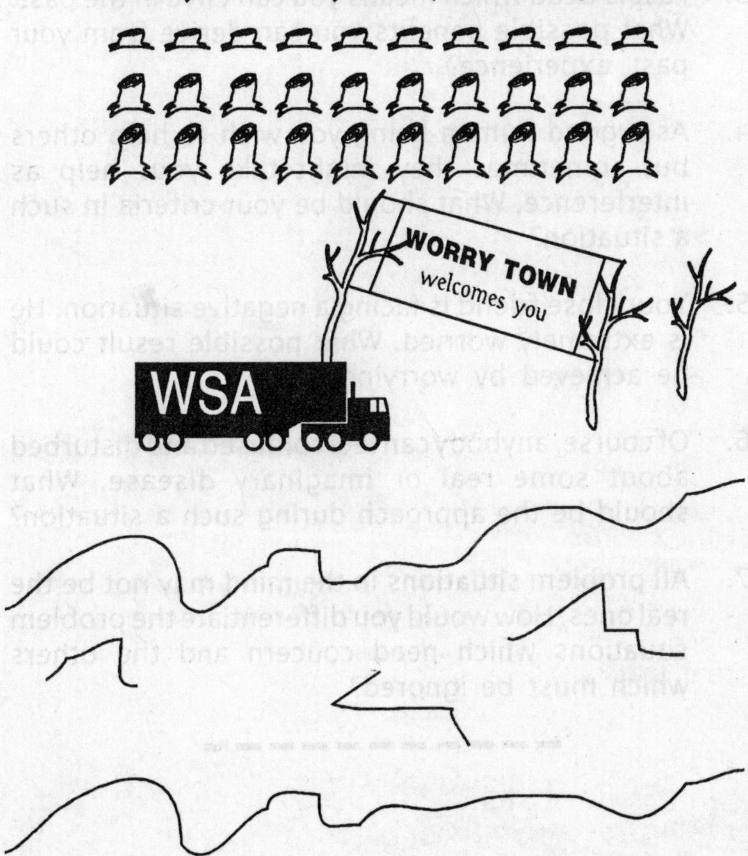

Explore Yourself

1. Many people feel that worrying is an integral part of life and you can't find the escape till the last breath. What is your opinion?

2. Out of your love and respect for somebody, you have promised to abandon one of your favourite activities. Are you comfortable? What could be the harm of suppression?

3. Past is dead which means you can't live in the past. What possible benefits you can derive from your past experience?

4. As a good human being you wish to help others but sometimes they might take your help as interference. What should be your criteria in such a situation?

5. Your close friend is facing a negative situation. He is extremely worried. What possible result could be achieved by worrying?

6. Of course, anybody can feel confused and disturbed about some real or imaginary disease. What should be the approach during such a situation?

7. All problem situations in the mind may not be the real ones. How would you differentiate the problem situations which need concern and the others which must be ignored?

Learning Objectives

By the end of this chapter, you will be able to understand that out of all worry situations :

- 40 % belong to future and never happen.
- 30 % are in the past which can't be helped.
- 12 % concern others, none of your business.
- 10 % are because of real or imaginary sickness.
- and 8 % are the real situations which are worth concern and must never be ignored.

All of us can conduct a worry survey of situations around us and even about others in our circle. These are not normal life situations but are those situations where we normally tend to worry. Many people feel that worry is a part of their lives but they forget that many of our life situations need not cause us any worry or even concern.

40% Never Happen

Out of all the so called worry situations, surprisingly 40% are the ones which we never face in reality. We are normally mentally prepared for these situations as we are afraid that these might happen. In the process we remain totally occupied in the imaginary negative consequences and indeed spoil our beautiful present. Thus, the present is full of anxiety, fear and all similar negative feelings. While performing in the present, we continue to be uncomfortable as if we would be caught red handed to face some unacceptable embarrassing situations or heavy punishment. This way our precious energy just goes down the drain. We remain fully unaware of the fact that only because of this folly of ours, we can sometimes actually get caught. Without anybody asking any questions we start replying. Even the other person feels confused and suspicious.

An idealistic father, on his son's admission to a professional college, gave him strict instructions " Now you are staying in the hostel, so concentrate fully on studies and never go to see any movie in a theatre. "The son promised. But there was a lot of difference in staying with the family and staying in the hostel. At times he felt home sick. He was feeling bored. All his friends were enjoying life; for them there were no restrictions. He felt like the odd one out. There is a limit to suppression of desires. For two years he didn't go to see any movies. Ultimately, the volcano was to burst.

One fine day he took a decision to study well and enjoy his life too. Since he had developed an image of a very reserved kind of person who is not interested in movies, he went alone to see a movie. He was feeling weak and nervous, he was afraid somebody might see him and complain to his father.

Anyhow he purchased the ticket and entered the hall. All the time he kept on feeling that his father was about to enter the hall from one gate or the other. Inspite of his best efforts to enjoy the movie he could not concentrate. Throughout he was developing a strong feeling, if his father couldn't come here he must be waiting for him in the hostel. The poor chap!

After the show it was with great difficulty that he reached his hostel. His pulse was very fast and his breathing heavy. Even while opening the lock he had a vague feeling that his father might be sitting inside.

He had gone to see the movie for enjoyment. He wanted to relax so that he could feel more energetic to study. He was worried about a situation in his imagination, which he didn't face at all. What did he get by worrying? He was experiencing the fear and mental balance was completely disturbed. It took him a lot of time and energy to revert back to his normal working level. Worrying could only give him heavy losses. It is very important to get clarity and plan precautions.

At the branch office of a multinational company, the manager was in a very cheerful mood when he received a telephonic message that the auditors were coming for inspection. Being a sensitive person, he felt panic. Immediately, he started going through all his records. He remained under heavy stress for three days till the auditors visited the office. He could neither sleep nor concentrate. Out of a total of twenty five, he could not prepare well even on one project. For the last six months, this project had been bothering him.

During their visit, the auditors had a superficial inspection of the branch and asked him certain general questions. The focus of the chief audit officer was not on finding faults but on encouraging the concerned officials by guiding them towards excellence for future performance. The poor manager remained disturbed till the team left. It took him literally two days to come out of his imaginary shock.

Here again the manager was worried about a situation which he never had to face. There is no relevance to plan, implement or even worry on those situations which we will never face in our life.

30% In The Past, Can't Be Helped

The next 30% are those situations which belong to the past. Today we are living in the present which by itself has no performance dependence over past situations. If in the past we had made blunders, that does not mean that today also only blunders will be committed. Similarly, if we have excelled in the past it does not guarantee our success today. We have seen people who did nothing for the last twenty years and now they are heroes. We have also seen those who were heroes earlier but are nothing today.

The past has no direct link with the present. Some worthwhile support received during past performances may not be available in the present. Life is a nonstop flow of time through various situations and events. No doubt the present is a part of this continuous flow from the past to the future but, at the same time, present is totally independent. Any desire to get a repeat of the past may not be fulfilled. Our desire or need may not be fulfilled on the expectation of, and false dependence on past strength. At the most, dependence is possible only on present resources and that too, those around us at a particular time. If our best resource is not available with us in the present moment, it is of no use.

PLEASE ! get up,
I need your help.
A Dead Man

The past is dead and it can't be revived. Even if we want something urgently from a dead person, it is simply not possible to get it. Still people keep on expecting from the dead. In the past they were dependent on that dead person. They want same old state of affairs to continue but the person concerned is no more available. In their mind they want to give repeated calls to that person as if more effort is required to make a dead person alive and active. Of course a person in deep sleep certainly needs more effort to be awakened. Further, there is a difference between a dead person and a person in a coma. A person in a coma looks like a dead person but in reality he is not. That person needs medical treatment and not repeated and loud calls.

For majority of people, unconscious (hidden) past experiences cause worry in the present : their present decisions are governed by some past experience. Can the past rule anybody? The past can never repeat itself. Then how can any decision purely based on the past be relevant? The past is no more. "Is it worth worrying over the past?" is a million dollar question. Because if it is beneficial, then every person must be motivated to worry and if it is not, we must train ourselves to stop worrying altogether. Even if we want to get something out of the past happenings, nothing is possible. It can't be helped.

Let us accept that past is of no use to us in the present. Any effort to revive our past is not going to succeed and will only lead to frustration. Under these circumstances we can very comfortably take a decision not to link the past with our present situation.

12% Concern Others None Of Our Business

70% of our worry situations have already been identified and the next 12% concern other people. Are they really none of our business? We do love others. We depend upon them for so many of our needs. We don't know when we might need the help of even strangers. Many a times, just to maintain or build up our relations, we extend our helping hand without even establishing our intention and competence to help. We simply presume that they will never seek our help.

Do others need our concern in their personal problems? At the same time, do we want others to interfere in our personal affairs? Do we really appreciate their show of concern? Of course we do want their help in our hour of need but we never feel comfortable if they start obliging us. We want them to help us only when we take a decision to seek their help and never as their decision to help us. We feel threatened if they take a decision to help us without being asked for.

Nobody in this world wants to be ruled by others. People prefer to suffer in silence than to expose their personal problems to others. Even in close relations people don't feel very comfortable to expose hundred per cent of themselves. We don't want others to come forward and help us unless we are feeling completely handicapped. We want to manage everything ourselves because we can't live under the pressure of obligations. The fact is that we need only a tip in the direction of help.

A lady had a sudden attack of high blood pressure. The doctor was called. What was the reason? When asked, she broke out, "Some students came in a group and mercilessly beat a professor staying in the next lane." She didn't know that professor personally. Without even assessing the situation she took it to heart and started worrying as if by doing so something positive would happen.

Like her, many of us have the habit of worrying about so many unconcerned and irrelevant issues. Without having any applying authority to solve a particular problem, we start putting our delicate mind on the problem. The fact is, we don't even have the slightest idea of relevant information. It is none of our business.

The same lady fully remembered how she felt alone in this world when her husband was in hospital. It was very difficult for her to arrange money for his open heart surgery. Facing problems at home, calling a doctor, taking a second opinion, getting admission to the hospital, going through all the investigations and at the same time looking after her job and small children – even today she trembles to feel those deadly moments. Nobody came forward for real help. Many people, without assessing their intentions, had just offered help but when requested, they silently disappeared. She had faith in many people in her circle but none came to her rescue.

The tragedy of our system is that people also shirk helping others. In their imagination they live the fear of total help required which they can't afford mentally and physically. What should we do when the problem belongs to the other person?

Establish Competence And Offer Help If Accepted Then Do It

First of all we must make an assessment at our own level, "Do we have the competence to help?" If yes, then just offer help. If we have the intention to help and if the other person feels the need of our help he will come forward. If we just start help without his consent, the other person who is already facing a problem, may feel highly embarrassed. People even say, " Why do you interfere in our affairs?"

10% Involve Sickness - Real Or Imagined

Next ten per cent are those situations which are caused by some sickness. If somebody has developed some problem in their circle, everybody else starts feeling as if he has also developed the same symptoms.

One boy studying in a medical college was feeling highly confused about the state of his health. Whatsoever was taught to him in the class, he felt as if he had the same symptoms. This way he became very depressed. Naturally, before joining the medical college he was hale and hearty but now he imagined he was suffering from so many deadly diseases. One day in the class he was taught about pregnancy. That was the height of it. He faxed his parents, " Help me, I think I am pregnant."

Of course, anybody can feel confused about some or the other imaginary disease. A person having a constant headache might start feeling as if he has a brain tumour; a person having pain and burning in the chest might think he has a heart problem and so on. Whether sickness is real or imaginary specialist doctors of all diseases are nowadays easily available.

On the expert's advice we must get all the investigations done and if required, start treatment. Many people don't go in for investigation out of an irrational fear. Their perception is that they will have diabetes if the report says, "Blood sugar is higher than the normal range." Does that mean if they don't go in for investigation, they won't have diabetes? For all our health problems, real or imaginary, specialized treatment is available; therefore, there is nothing to worry about.

Only 8% Is Worth Concern

Now we are left with only eight percent of those worry situations which keep us disturbed. These must never be ignored; otherwise, life will literally become hell. These are real situations which we are really facing in the present. Every such situation needs a very deep and thorough understanding.

If some student scores more than 75% marks in an examination, he is said to have got a distinction. Now, after all the calculations we have realized that 92% percent are those situations where no management is required. Thus we say that out of all our so called worry situations, we have scored 92% marks. It is something to celebrate. Now only 8% are left. Imagine the burden which has been laid off our minds. With all the energy and resources at our disposal this 8% IS NO PROBLEM.

This 8% is our logical problem, which we need to manage. The method to identify this eight percent, is very simple. Any problem which belongs to the present

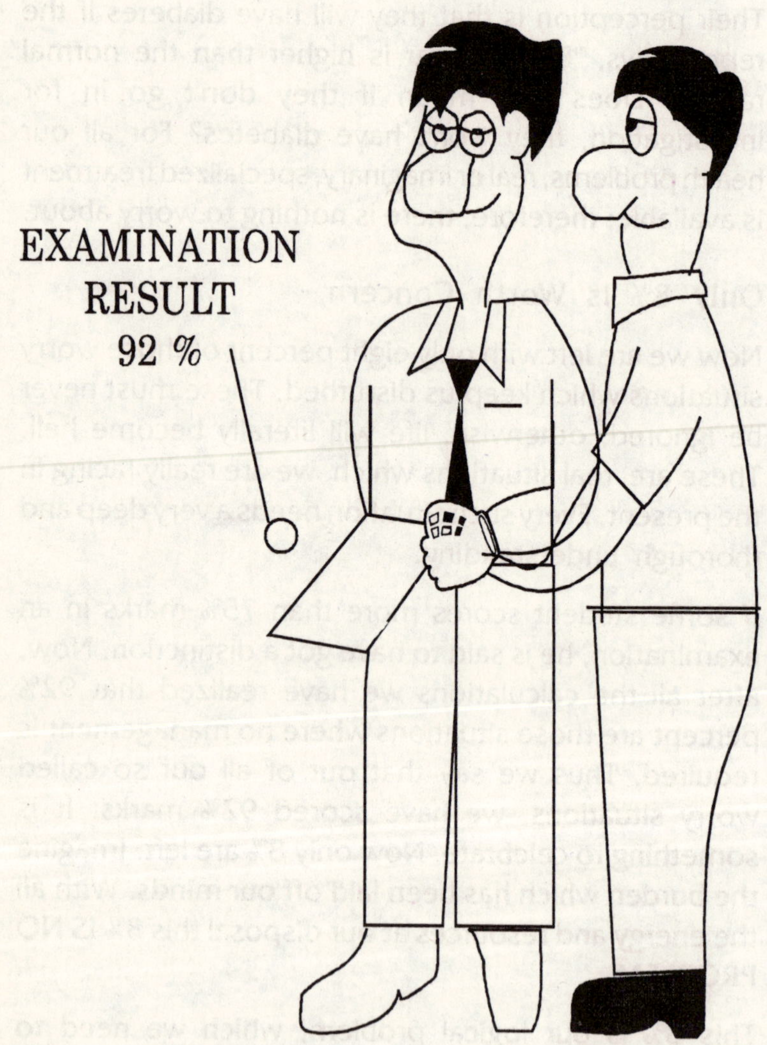
EXAMINATION
RESULT
92 %

falls under the category of 8%. The present, as we all know is not one year, one month, one week, one day, one hour, one minute or even one second. PRESENT IS JUST ONE MOMENT. Our focus must only be on managing the present moment.

Many people claim to live in the present still they remain disturbed. Their concept of the present is much beyond one moment. They feel that the present is either the whole life, or at least as long as this project is going to be completed. The project can be : marriage of their children, treatment of the parents, next promotion, completion of their house under construction or any other similar project. They do accept the present but also accept the future linked consequences. That's a blunder.

Once we identify present problems, our focus must be on gaining hundred per cent understanding of that. When we develop certain skills in managing those difficult life situations, even this 8% can also be easily managed, thus helping us lead a TENSION FREE life.

Purpose

To feel the harmful effects of attempting to live in the future.

What To Do

Make a list of ten situations where you were worried with some future link. Plan how to come back and live in the present in those situations.

Purpose

To feel the harmful effects of attempting to live in the past.

What To Do

Make a list of ten situations where you were worried with a link of your past experience. Plan how to come back and live in the present in those situations.

CHAPTER 7

HOW NOT TO WORRY?

TUG OF WAR

Explore Yourself

1. People normally tend to worry in most of the life situations. Does worry give you a positive or a negative feeling?

2. Most people confuse responsibility with worry. Do you feel disturbed with each and every responsibility you come across? Do you feel that worry is unavoidable when there is responsibility?

3. As a rule you don't waste anything in life, particularly when you are aware of it. Then why do people waste their much needed precious energy in worrying?

4. Many parents often feel responsible in warning their children, "I don't understand what you are doing? Your examinations are at hand; at least now start worrying." What should be your approach as a parent?

5. For a peaceful and happy living you must take a decision to practice not to worry. Where to find the opportunities for such a practice?

6. In their day to day expressions people are normally not clear about the use of the positive and the negative words. In your opinion what could be the possible benefit of using positive words?

Learning Objectives

By the end of this chapter, you will be able to :

- feel that worry is not a part of responsibility.
- realize as to how to invest your precious energy in justifying your responsibilities.
- undo the damage and move on to the track of becoming an expert on not to worry at all.
- identify the positive alternate expressions on the track of living a life free from worries.

It was the fourth consecutive meeting of all the board members in one month. The agenda was to re-discuss the new multicrore oil project with the group president.

"I feel nobody is worried how things are progressing. If the board members don't feel the stress of this new project, then how can the consultants, engineers and technicians?" said the worried group president in a disappointed voice.

"This clearly portrays that nobody around here is feeling the responsibility. Aren't you worried if the prestigious project is not completed in time. In that case we would be nowhere", he displayed more of his emotions in an endeavour to generate motivation. Like other three meetings this one also ended with an emotional lecture from the worried group president who completely forget his responsibility to discuss the constructive and essential details concerned with the project.

Most people confuse responsibility with worry. Do they really go together? Is worry unavoidable when there is responsibility? Do we feel disturbed with each and every responsibility we come across? Are we trained to worry from the very beginning? Has the journey of life and the journey of worry a common goal? Is there no escape from worry, or is it that we are not aware of such an escape? If a responsible person remains worried, can he carry out his responsibilities? Has worry no role while carrying out responsibilities or is worry an integral part of responsibility?

The answers to these questions may further confuse us if we don't have the clarity. It is very important for us to know whether worry and responsibility go in opposite directions or if they go parallel. If we feel they go parallel then worry seems to be equally important and should never be ignored. But if they go in opposite directions then living with worry is a dangerous arrangement. Does worry give us a positive or a negative feeling? When we examine all such situations, it becomes very clear that whenever we have worried, we have definitely felt negative only.

When we look back on all the responsibility situations, we have received only a positive feeling. If we avoid worry, our feelings about responsibility are always constructively positive. It fills in us a deep feeling of motivation and confidence. Mind is totally free from disturbances. We enjoy a sound sleep. We get up fresh in the morning. Our team members love to work with us. Accordingly, the results are also positive.

Investment or Speculation

Investment means we place money or energy in some activity so that it will increase in value. Only a person who is responsible will have a focus on investing. He knows very clearly what his needs are and what he can afford. If there is a losing proposition, he is fully aware of it. He will label that project as his research and development.

The word responsible itself reflects the meaning, "It is the ability to respond to any given situation to its desired level of management." Accordingly, every step has been well understood, assessed and planned thus, we have full control over all operations.

Whenever we spend money or energy in hope of getting the profits it is called speculation. In speculation we may get profits, but there are equal chances of loss also. In the event of loss, probably the project at hand was not felt in depth. The effort was made without proper planning. Needs and desires alone don't ensure profits. Unless they are backed by effective goal setting, proper understanding, planning, organizing and well guided performance, they are not very helpful.

Our aim must be very clear to us. The moment we have a clear cut focus on our well directed aim, we perform on the responsible track. And when the aim is not in focus, we invite worries. Responsibility always gives us comfortable positive feelings while worry only gives us uncomfortable negative feelings. The fact is.......

Worry and Responsibility Go In Opposite Directions

Worry and responsibility should go only in opposite directions as their being together is dangerous for our health and peace of mind.

Limited Source Of Energy

Let us not forget that we have a limited source of energy. Performance needs energy. Without energy nothing can move in this world. Whether we work in office or at home, whether we walk or talk, energy is required. Without energy we can't even listen or think.

Worry is indeed a mental process, so it also needs energy. On worrying, our energy is diverted towards worry and is wasted. We do need our precious energy to carry out our responsibilities. Worry is negative while responsibility is positive. This lands us into a tug of war like situation where two groups of people pull a rope in opposite directions. In this game, the winner is declared only when the energy of one side is out-balanced by the other. Similarly both worry and responsibility are pulling against each other. In the process the precious energy meant to carry out the responsibility is just being wasted in this tug of war.

For developing a clear understanding, let us consider a hypothetical situation. If 20% of our energy has been diverted to the worry side, then, as a simple mathematical equation 80% is left on the responsibility side. But it does not happen like that. So here also, to balance the situation, worry will snatch away 20% more energy from the responsibility side. Thus, we will be left with only 60% of our energy and not 80% as perceived earlier.

When we are investing only 60% of our energy the results will be proportionately lower. Normally, the person is not aware of this invisible loss and keeps on blaming luck or other factors for his poor performance. The fact remains that, in this case, 40% of our precious energy has been wasted, only because of worry.

ENERGY

WORRY (Waste) ↙ **RESPONSIBILITY (Investment)** ↘

20% ← 20% ← [80%] 60%

50% ← 50% NIL

MIND CAN'T FUNCTION

100% ← 100% FROM BODY'S RESERVE QUOTA OF ENERGY

FEELING LIFELESS

If, by chance, 50% of our energy has gone to the worry side, then it will snatch away 50% energy from the responsibility side. As a result, we will be left with no energy to perform. Without energy even the best of electronic equipments can't function. So here also our mind, which in the past, has been proved to be very sharp and intelligent, cannot function. We have all faced this kind of situation sometime or the other in life. We do say to ourselves, "What has happened to me! I cannot find a solution even for this very simple problem." We feel highly embarrassed within ourselves.

What happens when, in extreme negative situations, 100% of our working energy goes to the worry side. It needs an equal amount of energy to balance. It snatches away energy from the liver which is the body's energy reservoir. Then, we literally feel lifeless. We don't have the energy even to ask for a glass of water.

Luckily, the body's recharging system is very active and we start reverting back to our normal state. It is a pity that we don't even know the cause of this heavy regular loss. Imagine a servant who is stealing from your house regularly and you are not aware of his intentions and actions. What will ultimately happen is only a matter of common sense which, even a child can foresee.

Are We Intelligent?

The fact is yes, we are all intelligent. Our past record proves it. We don't need a certificate from a consultant. We already know that, as a rule, we don't waste anything in life, particularly when we are aware of its importance. We have never torn away a five rupee note. Then, why are we wasting our much needed precious energy?

The tragedy of the system is that there is no external source of energy: it must come from within. There is a false feeling that we can buy energy from external sources, e.g., through material comforts, by appointing consultants, or hard working and intelligent subordinates. To manage them effectively we again need energy. Otherwise, the moment others feel that we are in the habit of wasting our energy in worry, they

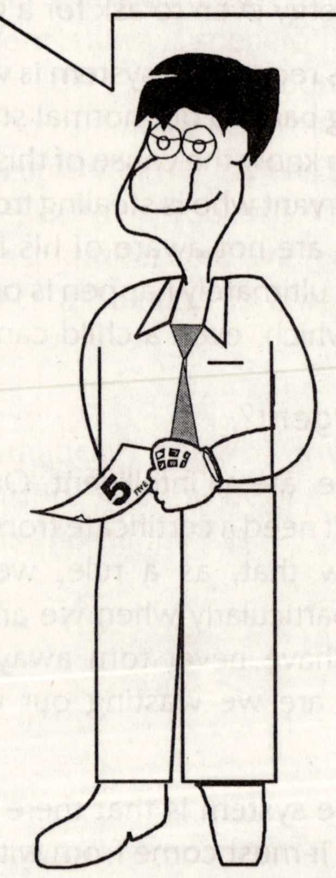

YOUR WISDOM SAYS
NEVER WASTE
YOUR PRECIOUS ENERGY
IN WORRY

will lose respect for our authority. Their focus will shift from their work to extracting the maximum from our resources for their benefits. Gradually, we will be shocked to see them flourishing in some other job or in their own business as our competitors.

Formally Trained To Worry

By now we know our energy is wasted in worry; so, our wisdom says, " It is precious, don't waste it, instead invest it in responsibility. " Simply by knowing that worry will squeeze away our energy is not enough. Over the years and, even for generations, we have been formally trained to worry. Even during early school days our parents warned us a number of times , " I don't understand what you are doing. Your examination is at hand; at least now start worrying. " Similarly, in performing any family or business responsibility, we have been forced to learn the damaging art of worrying.

Today we feel independent and free to take our own decisions. But are we really independent? Aren't we trapped from all sides by our deep rooted worrying habits? Can anybody change in one moment? Again, our desire alone is not enough. It must be backed by proper understanding and planning.

We know that practice has made us experts in the art of worrying. Now we need to undo the damage and move on to the track of becoming an expert on not to worry at all. Let us plan to reverse the process. As simple is always powerful, while the complicated is bound to be weak, focus on a simple method to become an expert.

Practice Not To Worry

As practice generates permanence we must take a decision and practice not to worry. For any kind of practice, we need opportunities made available to us. Where to find these opportunities? God is very kind to us. We are lucky. Everyday we face so many worry situations. In the morning when we get up there is no water in the tap, the child has missed his school bus, the wife is sick, the car is punctured, in the office maximum staff is on leave, we are not prepared for an important business meeting and so on.

We can take a decision to practice not to worry in all such situations. Life is full of problems leading to worries. So, everyday we have so many worrying situations or, let us say, the opportunities to practice not to worry. While facing such a situation just remind yourself, "I must not waste my precious energy in worry but instead invest it in responsibility." For example, if 80% of our energy is normally wasted in worry then, this time, it will be at least 1% less. If, on the average, we practice ten times a day then in an year it is 3,650 times. Maybe after about an year we will have developed a non-worrying personality.

Now the question is, if we don't worry, then how should we respond to the situation? What is the positive alternative to this negative and dangerous word worry?

As The First Practical Step, Use A Positive Word CONCERN, Instead Of Worry

The moment we use a positive word to express our feelings, we start feeling positive from within. "I am worried about my results" is replaced by, "I am concerned about my results." Similarly, "I am worried about my daughter's marriage" is replaced by, "I am concerned about my daughter's marriage" and so on.

In addition, let us take a decision to identify all the negative words we use in our daily life and identify the positive alternatives. "I have to reach my office by ten". What is the compulsion? It can be easily replaced by a simple and positive expression, "I must reach my office by ten or I should reach my office by ten or even I need to reach my office by ten". All these simply give us positive expressions and protect us from all the negativity of life.

Purpose

To feel that worry is not a part of responsibility.

What To Do

Make a list of ten of your responsibilities. Do you normally feel worried in all such situations? If not, then what are the reasons for not worrying? Apply the same principles in other worry situations.

Purpose

To identify positive alternate expressions on the track of living a life free from worries.

What To Do

Identify ten situations where you use negative words. Plan possible positive alternatives and feel the difference.

___

___

___

___

___

___

___

___

___

___

___

___

___

___

___

___

___

___

CHAPTER 8

DETERMINATION TO LIVE

Explore Yourself

1. What is the specific role of personality and character in sound health and in the development of ill-health? Compare and contrast.

2. Generally patients with deadly diseases may demonstrate three main types of attitudes. The first category of patients have an aggressive attitude towards cure. The second have a bland denial of the disease. The third have an attitude of hopelessness and helplessness. Which one of these you would recommend to sick people? Give reasons for your answer.

3. In your opinion, what is the specific role of Stress Management in the treatment of hypertension (High Blood Pressure)?

4. Why do most people, while appearing for an examination, just before an interview, or some challenging situation, experience minor digestive upsets or diarrhoea?

5. Out of a group of people having problems, how would you identify a person suffering from depression?

6. It is normally seen that depression reduces the ability of an individual to cope with life. What steps would you suggest to bring a person out of depression?

Learning Objectives

By the end of this chapter, you will be able to understand that :

- stress can be the main aggravating factor in certain chronic and even deadly diseases.
- inability to cope with life's demands results in depression.
- determination to live and a more hopeful attitude towards life can do wonders.

Long-term stress results in ill-health which can take the form of physical or mental disease, or both. Stress, and the way the body adapts to it, is one of the major causes of chronic illnesses such as heart and circulatory disease, hypertension, asthma, rheumatoid arthritis, eczema, migraine, depression, colitis, duodenal and gastric ulcers and, digestive dysfunction in general. A link is also suspected between mental states related to stress and the development of cancer although, it's by no means the only cause of any of these conditions. There's often an inherited tendency towards a specific problem and other factors, including unbalanced diet, lack of exercise and various infections are also involved in the development of chronic diseases. Stress, to which the body is exposed and the way our body reacts, often depends upon personality traits. There is mounting evidence of the role of personality and character in the development of serious ill-health.

How a person takes to a particular disease is very important in the aggravation or management of that disease. People who take disease as something that was bound to happen and happily accept it as such, have been seen to develop their spiritual powers. But others who took disease as something deadly have invited and welcomed those uncomfortable moments of life.

Deadly Diseases

It has been seen that chronic anger, disappointment, fear and the inability to cope with misfortune, all play a role in the aggravation of chronic and even deadly diseases. Further research into the attitudes of such patients has shown that they develop a tendency to dwell on past bereavements and real or imagined misfortunes. They also seem to have little sense of the future when compared with other patients who are seriously ill but not suffering from any chronic disease.

Such people have often been buffeted by fate, having endured a series of personal shocks and emotional disasters. Indeed, some psychologists have gone so far as to describe certain chronic and deadly diseases as "a socially acceptable way of committing suicide" : a way of escaping from the stresses of life without intentionally destroying oneself. However, while this may be true of certain patients, it's certainly not true of all. There is a need for such patients to display intelligent and positive cooperation in their treatment. Some patients, for no obvious clinical reason, made better recoveries than others. For a healthy recovery they must possess.....

Determination To Live And A More Hopeful Attitude Towards Life

Generally, these patients demonstrate three main types of attitudes. The first is an aggressive motivation towards cure. Here the patient is totally cooperative. Through well directed efforts, he has established total faith in the doctors. He is living a state of total acceptance and surrender. His mind is totally free from all pressures. Because of a situation of no stress, there is no negative effect on the recovery from the disease.

The second is a bland denial of the disease. These patients again don't carry any stress on their mind. But because of denial they also tend to ignore proper medical treatment. Recovery in such cases is slower than in the above category. It is surprisingly seen that because of no stress there is no aggravation of the disease. Here, the body's own defence mechanism comes into the picture and the patients start recovering even without proper treatment.

The third category of patients has an attitude of total hopelessness and helplessness. These are the worst kind of patients. They have no faith in the medical team and they feel completely helpless. Stress in these patients is at a peak. All the time they keep on feeling the deadly end moving towards them. They have lost interest in life completely. They contribute nothing to society, self or the family except for tension and misery.

Hypertension

Stress plays a more obvious role in some conditions than others. In patients having high blood pressure, for instance, long-term stress results in the quite

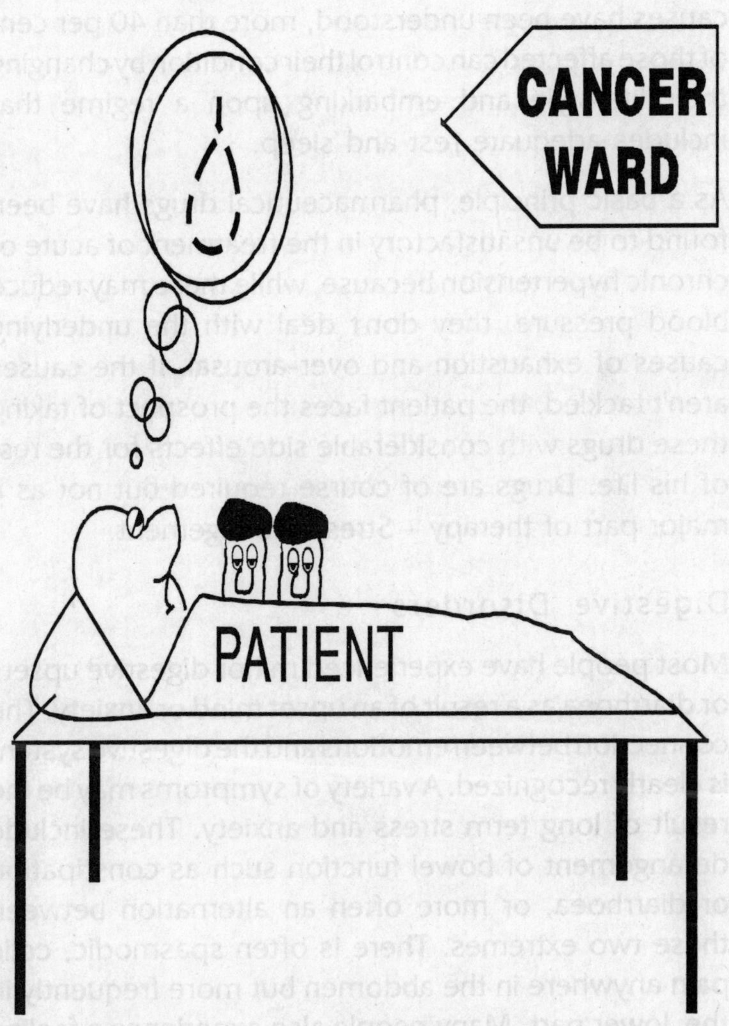
CANCER
WARD
PATIENT

normal raising of blood pressure. This is more so in response to any stimulus becoming chronic, simply by virtue of constant repetition. However, once the causes have been understood, more than 40 per cent of those affected can control their condition by changing their life-style and embarking upon a regime that includes adequate rest and sleep.

As a basic principle, pharmaceutical drugs have been found to be unsatisfactory in the treatment of acute or chronic hypertension because, while these may reduce blood pressure, they don't deal with the underlying causes of exhaustion and over-arousal. If the causes aren't tackled, the patient faces the prospect of taking these drugs with considerable side effects for the rest of his life. Drugs are of course required but not as a major part of therapy – Stress Management.

Digestive Disorders

Most people have experienced minor digestive upsets or diarrhoea as a result of an upset mind or anxiety. The connection between emotions and the digestive system is clearly recognized. A variety of symptoms may be the result of long term stress and anxiety. These include derangement of bowel function such as constipation or diarrhoea, or more often an alternation between these two extremes. There is often spasmodic, colic pain anywhere in the abdomen but more frequently in the lower part. Many people also experience a feeling of unexpected abdominal fullness and nausea. Another common symptom is difficulty in swallowing and a feeling of a "lump in the throat". These symptoms are often accompanied by other evidences of stress.

Once an organic disease has been diagnosed and obvious dietary factors have been eliminated as a cause, the most successful treatment of these conditions begins with a discussion of the life-style of the person and any stressful relationships. This can be done with an understanding friend or doctor. The next step is to bring about practical improvement in the life-style and normalizing stress causing relationships. Drug therapy in such cases is on the whole disappointing. It's important for the patient to realize that his condition is not "all in the mind" simply because there's no evidence of actual organic disease. Sometimes, it is observed that a visibly functional or psychological case may end up in some organic problem. Gastric/duodenal ulcers are the most obvious examples of early functional problems developing into organic lesions. It becomes very important to diagnose all organic problems through well directed investigations.

Clinical Depression

Reactions to stress are frequently the underlying cause of clinical depression. In this state, the mind of the patient is totally withdrawn. Any effort on the part of the concerned patient to regain normal health becomes impossible and professional help is necessary. Relevant symptoms may range from palpitations, a tingling sensation in legs and arms, hot flushes, headaches, digestive disturbance and lack of appetite to uncontrollable weeping and a tendency towards intense self-pity or self-blame.

Inability To Cope With Life's Demands Results In Depression

Depression will almost certainly reduce the ability to cope with life. People can become depressed when they distort events. They draw illogical and unfavourable conclusions by blaming themselves. A great deal of stress is the result of a mismatch between the physical and psychological demands of life and the individual's ability to deal with them. It is indeed a mismatch that in turn, often stems from a discrepancy between the world as it is and the world, as the individual feels, it ought to be. Life's demands seem to be multiplying, resulting in an unmanageable clash between imagination and reality.

Some cases of depression can be thought of as a way of opting out of what is seen as an intolerable situation. Collapsing into a depression appears to be one of the ways of avoiding the problem. The act of suicide is an even greater act of avoidance. Many people in uncomfortable situations enter into a self imposed depression just to gain sympathy and escape responsibility.

Depression causes changes in behaviour as the person attempts to cope. Then the new behaviour replaces the normal pattern of behaviour and may be accepted by those near to the individual. It may attract sympathy and may, in consequence, be more difficult to change. Phobias and neuroses can grow out of such a situation. If, because of anxiety, a particular situation is avoided, then a phobia might well develop by repetition of this action. "I might faint, therefore I won't go out where people might see me" results in avoidance of going out. The same (unconscious) thought, repeated each time when the possibility of going out of the house for any purpose is mentioned, results in an intense fear of going out, a phobia. The true fear is perhaps of fainting and making a spectacle of yourself, but the fear becomes transferred to going out.

Understanding the cause of this type of irrational fear is part of the cure. The actual cure comes only when the individual learns to modify his behaviour. Under close and caring supervision he is encouraged to do gradually what is feared. When the patient feels that no harm results, his fear automatically goes away. This takes time, perseverance, the use of relaxation of mind and other relevant exercises.

Depression can also be caused by a chemical imbalance in the body. Drug therapy can control this clinical depression known as endogenous depression. In this case, drugs are the only effective means of control; even then there's a likelihood that the illness will recur. In the long run, in cases of clinical depression, coming to terms with reality will only bring about a cure. Regular counselling or psychotherapy may be required to effect self-understanding and a complete recognition of the relationships between behaviour, attitudes and stress.

To sum up, although stress can't be pinpointed as the sole contributory factor in chronic illnesses and various disorders discussed above, it does play a major role, in some cases influencing the duration and direction of the illnesses. It makes sense, therefore, to recognize this potential for harm and to take steps to counter stress and tackle it positively. When the early stress signs appear, the chance for successful remedial action is at its best. When a breakdown, either physical or mental, has occurred, the task is harder and expert professional advice is essential. Even then, however, there's still an enormous amount we can do. Indeed, there's always something which we ourselves can do if we are prepared to make the effort.

Under all circumstances we can have a determination to live. Accept the situation as it comes. Remember, the ideal is rarely available. Plan what we can get out of the present resources so that we can live happily and peacefully. After all, it's our life.

Purpose

To understand that stress on an individual can be the main aggravating factor in certain chronic and even deadly diseases.

What To Do

Identify ten patients suffering from some deadly disease, five of them from a stressful environment and five from a relaxed and supportive background. Study their progress and feel the difference.

Purpose

To understand that determination to live and a more hopeful attitude towards life can do wonders.

What To Do

Identify ten chronic patients. Understand their respective life situations and give them a purpose to live. Follow up and feel the difference.

CHAPTER 9

I CAN DO IT

Explore Yourself

1. How is it possible to alter circumstances to reduce stress?

2. Stress in your life may have been caused by circumstances or the people around you. Who should accept the responsibility of managing it?

3. Tranquilizers should be taken only under strict medical supervision and that too for the shortest period of time during an emergency. Why do many people take them, on their own, resulting in addiction?

4. Normally people decide to forget their sour and bitter relations. How can a relation which has caused harm to them be over, simply by an attempt to forget? Explain.

5. One of the key causes of stress is living with uncertainty. It's always advisable to take appropriate action when confronted by a clear cut situation. How would you convert a situation of uncertainty into something clear, specific, and manageable?

6. Many ambitious people concentrate only on the end result and ignore the means. Do you agree or disagree? Give reasons to support your view point.

Learning Objectives

By the end of this chapter, you will be able to :

- learn how to cope with stress to minimize its health damaging potential.
- understand that in managing stress much can be achieved by planned personal effort.
- understand that it is not possible to forget anything in life, so you must learn to forgive.
- understand that change is unacceptable so the focus must be on developing yourself.

Our prime objective in effectively managing stress is to learn how to cope with it so that we can minimize its health damaging potential. Obviously, this task differs from person to person but certain steps must always be taken. The first thing to do is to identify the stress factors themselves and then, having done that, we must examine our attitude towards them to see whether our response is appropriate.

Are we over-reacting? To reduce stress, is it possible to alter circumstances? A close look at our personality and our overall vulnerability in terms of stressful events will help us identify some of the factors that are involved. The moment we understand ourselves and all the circumstances surrounding us, the management of stress automatically comes under control.

We have two areas to work in – internal and external. To improve matters internally, it's a question of altering attitudes and habitual responses through a thorough understanding and development of concepts.

To improve things externally involves altering, where possible, those aspects of life that cause stress. The key words in the last sentence are "where possible" because, as much as anything, it's the ability to accept what can't be changed, e.g., parents, bitter experiences, that enable a person to stay sane in a world full of potential hazards.

Once those things, over which we as individuals can exert no direct control, are removed from the scene, then it's possible and necessary to take a sensible look at the problems that remain and can be solved. These problems may involve feelings of uncertainty and doubt, a long-held feeling of resentment or hatred, lack of purpose, difficulty in personal relationships, inability to make decisions, or indeed any behavioural pattern that produces unhappiness.

Individual Responsibility

Many systems and methods have been evolved that attempt to unravel the confused emotions that prevail increasingly as a result of stress. And although planned counselling and advice are often necessary, much can be achieved by personal effort. Indeed, in the end, it's up to ourselves to solve our own problems, since the insight therapy and guidance given still need to be used by us. Above all, the reduction of stress simply remains a matter of gaining greater insight into our character, personality and habitual responses.

ATTENDENCE CHART

All Absent

1 Present

It's my Responsibility

Acceptance of the responsibility for dealing with our problems is a prime requisite for developing awareness and a full personality. For some, this means simply adjusting or reorganizing their life style, for others, it involves delving more deeply into spiritual areas and finding purpose and meaning beyond everyday life. Whether we plan to do the former or the latter, we will be in a position to make a start only when we have recognized and come to terms with the need for change and positive effort.

Drugs

The use of drugs to control symptoms should only be taken as a short-term measure. Their use for a few days or so, to help overcome a crisis, is justifiable, but beyond that there are risks. Simply masking stress symptoms will lead to more serious health problems, including the possibility of side effects. Tranquillizers are known to give a wonderful feeling. These drugs should be taken only under strict medical supervision and that too for the shortest period of time during an emergency. Some people take them on a long term basis, on their own, resulting in addiction.

Medical research has also shown that if any particular symptom of a chronically anxious patient is relieved by drugs, something else crops up to take its place, simply because the underlying cause was different.

Dispelling Uncertainty

One of the key causes of stress is uncertainty. It's always easier to take appropriate action when confronted by a clear cut situation. For instance, let us say, we lose our job. What do we do? Go out and look for some other job. Of course, it may not be easy to find work but the immediate question has a simple answer, we know what to do, we can at least try. But if the problem is merely a rumour about jobs being cut back, the uncertainty creates stress, we have sleepless nights and are unable to perform at our best. Ironically, the chances of our losing the job become even greater.

Having identified the source of stress as uncertainty about the job, the first step towards overcoming it is to plan a course of action, such as contacting other firms or job agencies, exploring the possibility of a job; or making a firm mental resolve to shelve the problem until there's a chance for more appropriate action. It's important to do one or the other and not merely worry obsessively and speculate endlessly. Taking action immediately reduces stress and this is true whether the action is going to a job agency or shelving the problem because, no appropriate or further action is possible for the time being.

To take another example, a swelling appears on the breast, causing anxiety, uncertainty and panic. Most such swellings are totally harmless but not knowing the cause can lead to intense stress. The result is a decline in our well-being and even more mental turmoil. The answer is to get a diagnosis done. Remember.....

Once The Enemy Is Identified, Appropriate Measures Can Be Taken

Learn To Forgive

Long held resentments, grudges and hatreds relating to real or imagined upsets, often in the past years, generate a great deal of stress. One way of releasing the tensions locked up in these emotional prisons is by "forgiveness therapy". If the very thought of someone results in a marked degree of tension, there's probably a case for forgiveness. In the first place, it's important to realize that what happened, lies in the past, which cannot be changed. Secondly, we must also recognize that by holding on to a negative emotional charge about some past happening, we harm only ourselves.

Whatever the circumstances, it's always possible to wipe the slate clean and forgive . Our common reaction to such a suggestion can be, "But I don't want to renew the contact. That relationship is over and done with." The truth is that the relationship is alive as long as it continues to maintain such negative emotional power. It will be over and done with only when the emotion resulting from the possibility of such contact is one of indifference. And this will happen only when the other party has been forgiven.

It is also a fact that it is not possible to forget anything in life. The more we try to forget, the more that idea or the person disturbs us. The only possibility left with us, to lead a happy and peaceful life, is to forgive. After forgiveness that idea will never disturb us because it becomes totally irrelevant in our life. The degree of tension released this way can be truly phenomenal.

There was a small happy family – Husband, wife and a two-year old son. If anybody wanted to see life, all they needed was a visit to that home full of love and happiness. Dining out at least once a week was their custom to break the monotonous routine. On one such evening when they were coming out of the restaurant, the husband asked his wife to wait as he went to get his car which was parked across the road. While he was in the middle of the road, he got run over by a car which went out of control.

The wife was terribly shocked. It seemed as if the happy smooth life had come to an end. She could not forget that horrible scene, particularly the driver of that ill fated car. All the time she had been living with a feeling of revenge and anguish. She filed a criminal suit against him. Sixyears passed and the case remained undecided. She spent all her savings in fighting the case. What did she gain? Practically nothing. And what did she lose? Well fleny! Her peace of mind, physical health, proper upbringing of her only son, respect in her social circle and the source of income which could not take proper shape when all the responsibilities came to her after his untimely death.

While discussing with her close friend she realized that the driver of that car had no intention to kill her husband. He was innocent. He lost control while driving because the brakes failed. Even he had been coming to the courts for the last six years out of compulsion. A punishment for no fault of his. Couldn't she forgive the person who was actually innocent, accepting that the accident was actually an accident?

She could now see that it was only an accident and not an attempt to kill. Understanding the whole situation, she decided to forgive him and withdrew the case.

She also realized that she had totally neglected her prime responsibilities towards her son, family members and her life. Her mind was feeling at peace and she could now concentrate on her career and education of her son. As a result she commanded respect in her own eyes and in her social circle.

Past, Present and Future

The past is an area in which many people stay trapped emotionally; it's essential to escape this trap and to concentrate on the present, which is, after all, the only time we are really alive. The future, too, can dominate the present. Since we are as much a product of our expected future as we are of our past, let us look forward positively (goals), live in the present and accept what can't be changed.

Once we have drawn up our goals, the next step is to plan how to attain them. There's a tendency to expect instant gratification of wants and desires. And if the desire, whether for a holiday or an automatic washing machine, remains unfulfilled, envy, resentment and anger can fill the mind. If appropriate measures, such as regular savings, haven't been taken to reach the goal, the all important means of achieving the end have been neglected.

Anger Is Always Self Generated

As Such It Can Be Positively Used

Taking Stress Out Of Relationships

Maintaining relationships is a delicate phenomenon. Sometimes, we feel positive while, at other times, we feel highly negative and angry towards the other person.

Bottling it up is harmful because it can be one of the most potent forms of stress. Our relationships require that feelings, needs and desires are expressed in a direct, non-accusative manner. If tensions within a person are building up, it does no harm to express emotions strongly, but express them in a constructive manner and respect the other person's sensitivity. We must remember that nothing and no one, should make us angry.

It is important that, instead of an angry response, we make an attempt at non-critical self appraisal. Listen to what's being said, evaluate it and then, either change your behaviour or explain and justify it. Listening to and evaluating what is said will give us an insight into how other people see us and accepting the criticism, or explaining calmly why we don't accept it, will help us avoid stressful confrontation. Clarify areas of disagreement so that they're mutually understood. If changes can be made to achieve harmony, make them. If this isn't possible, the best solution to prevent further disharmony is to agree to differ.

It's worth remembering that whenever we behave in a certain way, we add strength to the motivating force behind our act. For example, if we react angrily to criticism, or fall into a sulky mood in response to real or imagined rejection, this will reinforce our belief that these are the correct responses. By changing the response to a more positive form of behaviour and by repeating it, we'll gradually come to adopt the new response as the correct one.

Making Decisions

Although there's no way of anticipating all possibilities, basic planning is a good first step towards good decision making. Start by writing down the nature of the problem and defining the choices that appear to exist. Don't forget one important choice, which is sometimes overlooked, the positive decision to do nothing. Usually, only a limited number of choices exist, so write down the merits and demerits of these. Having an ideal end results in mind help, so write this down as well. However, if after defining the problem and out of all the reasonable options open to us, no solution seems obvious, spend a little time doing some lateral thinking, looking for unusual solutions. You'll probably find in the end that you'll have to make a combination of solutions because there's seldom an ideal answer. Remember every decision once taken always needs modifications according to changing situations.

Take, for example, the case of a widow who lives alone and isn't well enough to take care of herself. She has two married children who live at different places. Both want her to come and live with, or near them. She believes that whichever child she chooses the other will feel neglected. What should she do? She could stay where

It's The Initial Indecision That Creates The Stress

she is, or go to one of her children. The combination of solutions would be to spend some time with each or to choose an alternative companion with whom to share her own home. There's no ideal solution, especially if she's uncertain whether her children genuinely want her to live with them; but it's essential to make a decision, to make the most desirable or, at any rate, the least undesirable choice.

It is very true. Many people are in the habit of not taking any decision in the very first place. What is the result? They remain wherever they were. Other people in their circle had taken decisions even if they were the wrong ones. After having chosen the wrong decisions, ultimately they succeeded in finding the right track of their choice. A wrong decision may initially entail some loss but, learning from failures, we ultimately get what we want in life. If we keep on hesitating in our initial decision making then we become stagnant in life. The drive or charm in our life will be totally missing.

Once a decision is made, stress is greatly reduced. It's important, too, to be positive about the decision once taken, while bearing in mind that there's always a room for modification if, for whatever reason, it doesn't turn out to be as successful as you'd originally hoped it would be.

Habits

To a large extent we are all creatures of habit. " Are our habits likely to reduce or create stress? As discussed earlier, it's easier to change our own self and our habits,

Change Appears To Be Unacceptable So Focus On Developing Yourself

It Is Practical

than to change the rest of the world. We have control only on ourselves: we can't change the system of our government, habits of neighbours, or even the spouse. Altering our personal habits so that we eat better, sleep better, interact better and exercise more. This will pay real dividends in terms of reduced stress, improved health and a good sense of well-being. Many of us are confused about changing our self so remember.......

It's worth noting here the role that exercise plays in stress reduction and improving health. Many people take no exercise at all, yet the body was designed for activity. As circulation is stimulated by exercise, the presence of lactic acid, which not only fatigues the body, dulls the brain and heightens anxiety, is reduced, while the production of adrenaline and noradrenaline, which can be linked with a general feeling of happiness and alertness, is increased. Although jogging round the block, or taking any form of exercise for that matter, won't solve all our problems, it will have an invigorating effect on both, the mind and the body, helping to banish lethargy and boredom.

Purpose

To understand that in managing stress much can be achieved by planned personal effort.

What To Do

Imagine yourself in ten stressful situations. What would be your personal strategy to manage?

Purpose

To understand that it is not possible to forget, so for comfortable living you must learn to forgive.

What To Do

Make a list of ten persons, you could not forget till today, who caused harm to you in the past. Take a decision to forgive them and feel the change.

CHAPTER 10

GIVE ME PROBLEMS, PLEASE!

Explore Yourself

1. Are problems blessings or a curse?

2. Many people have a firm belief that whatsoever God does is for the best. As per their belief, if a problem is a blessing then why do they feel bad when it comes?

3. In any organization, when there is some unmanageable situation, what criteria does the management normally adopt while selecting the officer for that responsibility?

4. When some experienced officer is selected, even for him it is an equally difficult situation. But he normally says, "Sir, I am feeling honoured". Why?

5. After passing class I, you didn't repeat the same, but preferred to go to class II. Certainly class II was tougher than class I. In many more life situations you have only preferred to undertake and perform something tougher than before. Does it prove your madness or wisdom? Why?

6. Why do many people say that problems are indeed blessings in disguise?

7. When you accept a problem as a blessing, how does it affect your attitude?

Learning Objectives

By the end of this chapter, you will be able to understand that :

- ❖ a Problem always comes in the present, but it has a strong link with the past and the future too.
- ❖ a problem is a compliment on the competence gained in the past, so feel honoured.
- ❖ a problem is indeed an opportunity to gain further competence for the future, so be thankful.

Normally, most people consider problems as a curse. Are they really a curse or do we have only a false feeling? Because we are confused about the status of problems in our life, we always remain disturbed while dealing with any problem situation. Whether they are blessings or a curse, we must know. If problems are blessings there is nothing to worry about. If by chance they are established as a curse, then let us accept the reality so that the mind does not go negative. Many people have a firm belief that whatsoever God does is for the best. The question is why these people feel like that. If problems are blessings why do these people feel bad when facing a problem.

A problem always comes to us in the present which is just one moment. It has a strong relevance in our life being a part of the continuous chain from the past to the future. For developing a deep understanding about problems, the past and the future cannot be ignored.

Link In The Past

Once a company accepted a tough project. In the board of directors meeting, every body was disturbed. What to do? Ultimately, they decided to call one of their dynamic executives. He had a track record of many achievements to his credit. The directors knew that for him also the present situation was a tough one to handle. He came to the conference room. Every aspect of that project was explained to him. The chairman said, "Now this project is your responsibility." The executive, with a smile of achievement on his face, said, "Sir I am feeling honoured."

Isn't it surprising that instead of feeling shocked and disturbed, he is feeling honoured? Why is he feeling like that? If this was a problem for his seniors, was he not receiving it as a problem? Was he more competent than all his seniors? Why were his directors feeling disturbed and not he?

At that moment he had not gone into the practical details of that situation. His only thought was that he had been selected out of so many in the company. There must be some reason. The board of directors must have noticed something remarkable in him. Based on his past performance, they must have got confidence in his competence. He was only establishing a link with the past as to why he had been selected. So, he was taking this as a compliment and not as a problem.

You 've to handle this serious problem
I'm honoured Sir !

Feel Honoured

Whenever a visible problem situation is given to us by anybody or it comes to us on its own accord, it is indeed a compliment to our competence which we have shown in the past. A person who has no competence is not selected to solve a problem. In our routine life, whenever we have some problem and need somebody's help, we determine his competence in our mind before sharing our situation with that person.

Similarly, when we receive the problem our competence has already been established by the person concerned or, say even by God. Silently those people are giving us a compliment. Firstly, they might not be aware about the compliment they are giving and secondly, their ego might also be coming in the way of declaring it as well-earned compliment. Have we ever felt disturbed while receiving a compliment? Isn't it an honour?

Link With The Future

A pleasant link with the past has been established and it confirms that the problem is indeed a blessing. But what is it's link with the future? We agree that recognition of our competence in the past, gives us a true and powerful feeling of honour. But aren't we supposed to face all those consequences in the future? After all, how can a problem be a blessing for the future? If we just keep the future in mind can our problems give us a feeling of comfort? Our aim is to grow in life and succeed at every next step. How can we achieve our goal surrounded by problems?

Let us look back at the good old days. When we passed class I, we didn't repeat class I, but instead preferred to go to class II. Needless to say class II was tougher than class I. Had somebody forced us to repeat class I, we would have felt insulted and humiliated. Even in early childhood we had all preferred to undertake something tougher than before. It seems as if we loved problems. Looks funny because at the same time we hated them.

Why to talk of our childhood, even today whether we are aware of it or not, we love the so called problems. After doing graduation we love to do post graduation, after establishing business at the local level we prefer to go to the state level, then to the national level and further, through exports, to the international level. Similarly, when we have established our business in one line, our next focus is on diversifying into even totally unknown ventures. In all these and many more situations we have only preferred to undertake and perform something tougher than before. Does it prove our madness or wisdom?

Mad? Certainly not. It only proves our wisdom. We feel proud of all these decisions of ours. Every situation which we label as a problem is indeed an opportunity to develop further competence for the future. It is human nature to keep growing. Life becomes dull when growth is stopped. In an office if we tell a person, " From now onwards you will not have any promotion. Just

TO DO TOUGHER THAN BEFORE IS THE ONLY WAY TO DEVELOP

keep on doing the same old mechanical job", what is the result? As there is lack of growth and lack of recognition, he becomes dull and gradually loses interest in his work.

Be Thankful

We don't want to lose our zest in life unnecessarily. We need opportunities to gain more and more competence for future achievements. It is a universal truth that doing something tougher than before is the only way to grow. So, whenever a problem or a tough situation comes, we must feel thankful for the opportunity given. Every problem, that we have accepted as an opportunity is indeed a step on the staircase of success.

The moment we treat every problem as a compliment and an opportunity, our whole attitude towards life undergoes a total change. Life remains the same but our previously negative attitude becomes constructively positive. Earlier, the focus was on avoiding each and every situation, but now the focus is on welcoming every opportunity. Earlier, our precious but limited energy was just being wasted but now our energy is being automatically recharged and invested. Earlier, we tended to blame others for our mistakes but now we gladly accept total responsibility for every situation. Why is it happening like this? Why is life now full of peace, energy and happiness? What could be the reason for this miraculous change? The fact is....

Blessings Come To Us In The Form Of Problems

Blessings always give us positive and uplifting feelings. So, under the cover of blessings, let us develop a clear understanding that the situations we face in life can either be easy, difficult, complicated, confused or even impossible.

Easy means there is nothing to worry about, start performing and get results. If the situation is difficult it may be because of our lack of competence in that subject. So let us start working to gain competence and it becomes easy. Remember, everything in life seems difficult before it becomes easy. So understand the situation and plan accordingly, then it is very easy to implement.

A situation can become complicated if it is entangled with many other situations. Overlapping of various solutions will obviously make it complicated. Dealing with only one situation at a time makes it easier.

When it is a confusing situation the focus must be on clearly understanding all aspects of that situation. It again becomes easy to implement. But if it is identified as an impossible situation, that means we lack the required resources. Take a decision not to take any initiative in that direction. This way we will find every situation as a blessing only and life will be totally free from all negativity.

Purpose

To feel that the problems you received are a compliment on the competence you have gained in the past.

What To Do

Identify ten situations from your past experience when problems were received as compliments. Assess the reasons and gain total depth.

Purpose

To understand that the problems you receive in life are in fact opportunities to gain further competence for the future.

What To Do

Make a list of ten problem situations from your past experiences and feel how these proved to be opportunities for you.

____

____

____

____

____

____

____

____

____

____

____

____

____

____

____

____

____

____

Chapter 11

PEACE OF MIND – NOW HERE OR NOWHERE

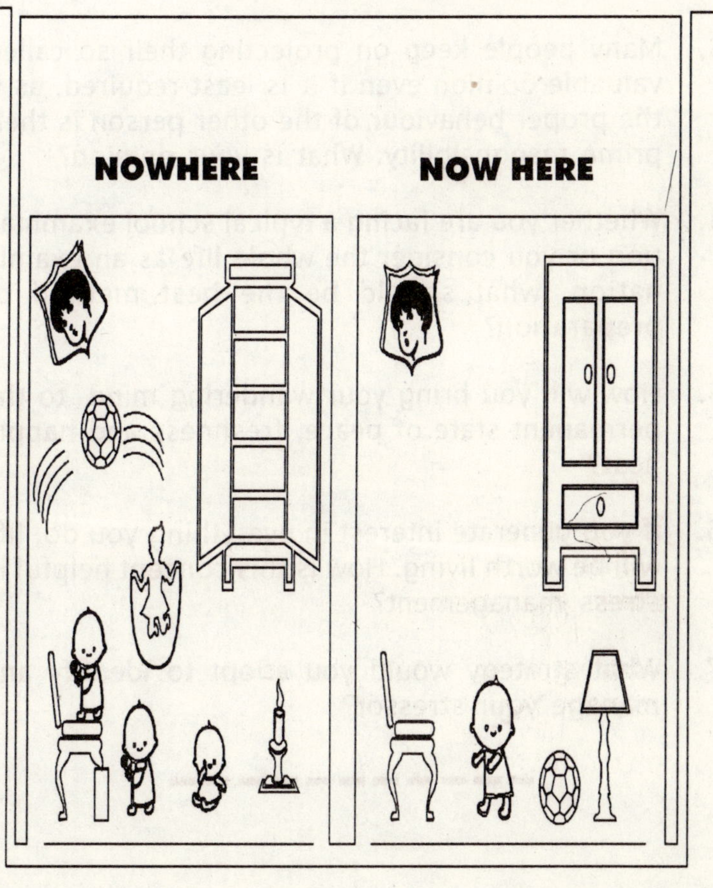

Explore Yourself

1. You can't escape stress. No doubt in certain circumstances, it can be avoided but it must never be ignored; otherwise, it can lead to serious consequences. Do you also think the same?

2. Why is it more important to identify the concerned stress factor and plan to manage it effectively, while many people only focus on exercise and relaxation techniques?

3. Many people keep on projecting their so called valuable opinion even if it is least required, as if the proper behaviour of the other person is their prime responsibility. What is your opinion?

4. Whether you are facing a typical school examination or you consider the whole life as an examination, what should be the best method of preparation?

5. How will you bring your wandering mind to the permanent state of peace, freshness and happiness?

6. If you generate interest in everything you do, life will be worth living. How is this concept helpful in stress management?

7. What strategy would you adopt to identify and manage your stressor?

Learning Objectives

By the end of this chapter, you will be able to :

- learn that stress must never be ignored.
- cultivate relaxation and confidence.
- decide never to test yourself but focus only to develop self understanding.
- to make and follow your stress chart.
- learn to maintain the status of permanent peace, freshness and energy of mind.

Peace of mind is what everybody aspires to have. In search of peace man visited temples, sacred places, went to the forests, tried meditation but could not find it. He hunted for it on the highest mountains. He even climbed mountains when he could bravely walk, searched every where, but in vain. The more he searched, the more he felt lost and the more restless he became. His search for peace ended when he looked into himself and realised that peace of mind is now here or no where. The letters "N O W H E R E" are same in both the expressions. Where you pause, infact, makes all the difference.

Stress, in certain circumstances, can be avoided but it must never be ignored; otherwise, it can lead to serious consequences. If a pigeon closes its eyes, the cat does not go away but will be in a better position to catch and eat the pigeon. Similarly, by ignoring stress we will only be inviting more problems.

Accepting stress itself is a positive move that relieves many pressures. If a speaker feels that everybody in his audience is a fool, he is making a fool of himself. It is as good as speaking to a wall. Very boring indeed. It will make the speaker feel nervous. For how long can a person speak effectively without any feedback from the audience? On the other hand if the speaker feels that the audience is intelligent and receptive he will be very comfortable in expressing himself without fear, anxiety or any such negative feelings.

Identify Self Stress Response

Knowing how to identify a stress response is similar to knowing when your car sounds "funny" or when the engine is "pinging." If we drive our car every day, we may be able to know when something is in need of repair, just on the basis of how it feels or sounds. If we have repaired the car ourselves, we may even know what is wrong. As in this example, the more knowledge about automobiles we have, the more likely are the chances to notice the changes and know if repairs are needed.

Similarly, the more we study our bodies and how they respond to stress, the more we will be able to prevent major stress problems. If, under pressure, we have been driving ourselves beyond reasonable limits, we may have the same trouble our car would have, if we always drove it all day at more than hundred kilometres an hour. We may not notice the little things that are going wrong which may lead to major problems. Likewise, if we get used to a strange sound or a racing motor, it may be hard to detect, even when we listen for it.

If, over a period of time, we have learnt to ignore our personal stress response, let us focus on studying our body's response during an exciting part of a movie or television show. We can also feel the stress response of others in this way. It is also possible while interacting with many people during our routine activities. Once we have seen some response in others then we also start feeling our own stress responses. This is like going for a drive to listen to your car.

It was observed in a stress management group for executives suffering from hypertension that many participants had increased blood pressure during the TV programs. On another occasion several executives began to monitor their blood pressure during the half time/interval of football games on television. Surprisingly, their blood pressures were significantly higher than before the game. To understand the true excitement of the game they then began using half times for their Sunday afternoon in practice sessions.

Realizing that stressful situations at work and home were having similar effects, they were asked to start monitoring their blood pressure levels and analyzing the stressor in their lives. It was suggested that they use coffee breaks and lunch hours to assess their stress levels and practise relaxation. Of course, one method is to do some exercise for relaxation but more important is to identify the stress factor and plan to manage it effectively.

Our body's response to an exciting show will help us understand what happens to our body when we are uptight. Much of the pleasure associated with watching a show is our emotional involvement as the actors realistically portray the drama. If we take time to notice, we may find our heart pounding during a chase scene or our stomach full of butterflies during a horror picture.

All this will keep on happening till we develop in-depth understanding of various life situations surrounding us. Once experienced, then same amount of excitement or suffering will not disturb us.

Being Uptight

Being uptight in the real world can produce discomfort and feelings of terror even greater than when viewing a horror film. Think of common everyday stressor such as traffic jams, deadlines, problems at work or quarrels at home. This is not an easy world in which to relax. In this era of stiff competitions we also become uptight. All the time we remain tense and function only from that base.

We keep on projecting our opinion even if it is least required. We also feel that it is our responsibility if the other person does not behave properly. We become judgemental. We feel in our judgement that the other person is a fool and we are very intelligent. We accept it as our prime responsibility to set him right so that he may not repeat that unacceptable performance.

In an unusually stressful situation, we may notice our emergency response as heart beating faster, muscles becoming tense and blood pressure soaring. But, all too often, our stress is slowly and steadily grinding away at us. Stress can never give us peace and happiness. But whenever we are under stress, we do experience some odd feelings.

The need to tackle symptoms of stress is the moment we feel them. Generally, many people stop listening to their stress warnings and may not realize how tense they have been until they start getting a daily headache which disturbs their routine.

An active executive may have 250 blood pressure peaks during each day until, eventually, his blood pressure stays up permanently. When we tend to ignore the first negative reaction then further negative reactions also start getting ignored till we develop a habit. The habit of being uptight is something we cultivate, no doubt without our planned effort.

If we assess how we have unknowningly cultivated the habit of being uptight, we can also get a direction on how to cultivate relaxation as a planned programme. Suppose we take a decision, " I will not get disturbed". When something happens which is disturbing then what to do? Is there some method not to feel disturbed. Earlier the focus was not to identify any other track. Once we rule out the negative path then surprisingly some positive or even approximately positive path starts becoming visible and gives us a feeling that ....

Relaxation Can Also Be Cultivated

Quiet Confidence

Imagine our heart slowing down, breathing becoming smooth and rhythmic and all tension slowly slipping away. Now, imagine someone rushing in to ask for an important decision. We slowly breathe in and slowly breathe out. As we do, our body relaxes and our mind clears of distractions and we make the decision calmly. This moment of relaxation is often seen by others as a sign of quiet confidence. Imagine how good it must feel to have cultivated such a habit.

One of the first steps worth making this form of relaxation a habit, is to recognize the habit of being uptight. Each of us responds to different stressors and stressors vary in the amount of response they trigger.

For example, a student may experience a great deal of stress when taking an examination in a subject he finds difficult or uninteresting. Before, during and after the test he may experience constant worry. The same student may respond in a totally different fashion to a test in his favourite subject. He may still experience stress in preparing for this test, but it will be less intense. He may go through the same activities to prepare for each test, but the emotional and mental stress will be different.

Whether we are facing a school examination or we take life as an examination, if we experience stress and get disturbed, our performance will be directly affected. In life, as a general principle, we can't afford failures. The best method of preparation will be...

Assess And Develop Self Understanding

Never Test Yourself

Emotional Frustration

In modern life, stress from emotional frustration is more likely to produce disease than physical stress. One famous cardiovascular surgeon is supposed to work eighteen to twenty hours a day. He is often on his toes and usually takes the stairs instead of the elevator to be sure he gets exercise. Although his schedule is hectic and demanding, he seldom becomes ill or experiences the effects of chronic stress. Why? Because he is not experiencing stress from his job; he is doing work he enjoys and finds it meaningful.

In our complex world, we may realistically find that not everything about our lives and jobs is as rewarding as we would like these to be. Sometimes, uninteresting jobs become frustrating. Retirement sometimes seems to be boring. Work may be good only if we achieve something meaningful by doing it. It may wear us out if we never seem to get anything done or if, what we do, is not important to us. At times marriage and family life are also frustrating and stressful. By learning how we respond to the stress in our everyday living, we will be able to learn how to respond differently in the future.

First, we must learn to recognize the stressors in our lives. If they happen to be part of our job, we must understand the importance of their role in the completion of the job. This way we will generate interest in that job. Once interest is generated we will never face any kind of boredom or frustration in life. If we generate interest in every thing we do, life will be worth living.

Twenty Four Hours Meditation

MEDITATION is a process to bring the mind to rest. Normally people force their mind to come to rest, which practically is not possible. For managing our life our mind must be peaceful, fresh and energetic all the 24 hours every day, throughout the life and not only for one minute or one hour or a day. Our focus is to develop a very clear concept on how we can bring our mind to the present moment and maintain the status of permanent peace, freshness and energy. This powerful level is attained by gaining the required depth in a simple and practical approach of Twenty Four Hours Meditation.

The mind of an average person is working all the 24 hours while legs, arms, tongue, eyes, etc., are used only when there is a need, otherwise they are resting but are very much there with us. If we keep on running and running, a time will soon come when we will feel totally exhausted and may even faint. Even if we don't faint, we are not fresh. In the same way, if the mind is used continuously it can lead to a nervous breakdown or the person may go insane. And even if we don't reach that stage, we are totally exhausted and not fresh. There is no peace and no energy left to work more. Basic need for the mind is freshness, peace and energy throughout our life.

Can we bring the mind to rest under force, as a conscious effort? Many people have tried but none could succeed, because it is simply not possible to bring the mind to rest under force. The force can be effective only for a short while and not as a life long process. Meditation is an automatic process to bring the mind to rest, which needs a logical and practical approach.

Feel a situation when we are sitting in our room and somebody knocks at the door. If we don't open, he will knock more and then more hard and still if the door is not opened the neighbouring people will collect outside with all their negative and confused feelings or the person will go back to bring with him more persons to force open the door. Earlier we were supposed to deal with just one person who was neutral or slightly negative, but now we are compelled to deal with a crowd of negative people. Same is the case with our mind. If we stop the entry of any idea under force it revolts back with the crowd of negative ideas which needs more of our energy. The best way is not to stop entry of the idea but to welcome the idea, assess it and then dispose it off either outside or inside the mind. Various files are managed in the computer.

In our office if we are to meet ten persons every day, one method is to have a joint meeting and all points are discussed till evening, with no conclusions and looking very busy all the time with no achievement. Other method is to plan one hour as meeting time. Meet people one by one, listen to their problems/ viewpoints, assess and then dispose off all ten persons within half or one hour. If the next person comes to meet us after two hours, we are practically free and resting till that time without any pressure of responsibilities. Similarly we must plan half to one hour every day for meeting the ideas which is indeed the MEDITATION. Welcome all the ideas and dispose them off one by one as a policy decision. Even if some funny idea comes, we must experience all the linked consequences in imagination or in reality, then dispose it off. There is often an overloading of ideas in the mind, so start welcoming them one by one. When one idea is disposed off on logics, many more relevant ideas are also automatically disposed off. With regular practice, within a couple of weeks or months we reach a stage when every idea is disposed off and we are practically free and fresh to welcome the next idea/problem for its desired level of management.

Let us see how this process is automatic. Running water is always fresh, so with regular flow of ideas, the mind remains fresh. But running water is not peaceful and does not produce energy. For getting energy a dam is planned on the running water which automatically leads to the lake formation. When we start disposing off the ideas, automatically the mind level is raised and the dam is installed on the flow of the mind and this way the lake of the mind is formed which is very peaceful. Whenever a new idea comes, the gates of the dam are opened and the relevant files in the computer mind release the information required, with full force and energy. The moment that idea or problem is managed, again the lake of mind becomes peaceful, fresh and ready for the next idea or the situation. This way the mind is tamed and remains at peace all twenty four hours and full of energy and freshness. It is now fully prepared to effectively deal with various life situations.

The word meditation has its origin from the word medicine. Every person is born intelligent. But our system of education and exposure to life makes people more unintelligent. Meditation is indeed a process to undo the damage caused to our mind over the number of years. As a simple expression, doing everything intelligently is meditation. That's only possible if our mind is totally free from all negativity and pressures of life and every desire have been logically accepted and fulfilled or logically rejected, which is only possible if we feel all the consequences attached to our desires in hundred per cent depth.

Your Stress Chart

Let us make a chart or a list of our current stressors. As we do, our list should grow and we become more and more aware of them. Remember in this world, no two individuals are alike : faces are different, voices are different, handwriting is different, finger prints are different, tastes are different, needs are different : then how can their stressors be the same, obviously they are also different. So every person will have his own list which will be different from ours.

To quantify how much current stress we experience, label it from 0 to 10 SUD (Subjective Unit of Distress). With 0 being no stress and 10 being the maximum we could imagine. Also, consider whether relaxation and controlling our body's stress response would be helpful. We may not find stressor such as noise, meeting people, pregnancy and bringing up children distressful.

We must list such stressor to understand all areas of stress in our lives. Other stressor we face may be managed through relaxation that can help us feel calm, balanced, or in less pain. Do update this list frequently by adding, removing or changing stressor. It is very important that we must plan and execute a regular follow up. This way our previous stressor will start disappearing gradually and the new one will find their place to be understood and managed. When every stressor has been properly identified and managed as a policy decision, we attain a state of everlasting peace.

Purpose

To feel that relaxation and confidence can also be cultivated.

What To Do

Make a list of ten stressful life situations. Plan your strategies how to get relaxed and generate your confidence.

Purpose

To identify the track on how to make and follow your stress chart.

What To Do

Make a list of your current stressors. Label it from "0 to 10" SUD (Subjective Unit of Distress). With "0" being no stress and "10" being the maximum you could imagine. Maintain the weekly follow up.

___

___

___

___

___

___

___

___

___

___

___

___

___

___

___

___

___

STEP TOWARDS

STRESS

ERADICATION

For The Organization

Every Person Must Be A Profit Centre

The corporate profit targeted is normally five times the salary given to the individual. If the monthly salary of an executive is Rs 50,000.00, then the daily salary would be Rs 2,000.00 and per hour salary would be Rs 333.33

So the corporate profit per executive for one hour would be Rs 1,666.50. The corporate profit per executive per hour for one year would be Rs 4,99,995.00 or say it is Rs 5,00,000.00. Thus the targeted corporate profit for 25 executives per hour for one year would be Rs 1,25,00,000.00.

If some organization is not earning this much profit, that means its operational systems needs re-orientation.

If because of any reason 25 executives are unable to contribute for one hour per day then the corporate loss for one year would be Rs 1,25,00,000.00. This huge loss is only a simple situation of non-contribution.

When the executive takes a wrong decision the loss is in multiplication. That is more visible in big organizations. The organization being big or small, as a responsible person you can not afford to take wrong decisions.

Live Responsibility Of The Level Of A Prime Minister

Just
One Wrong Word can Create a War Between Two Countries

In your case it may not be two countries but certainly two organizations or two departments or even two individuals. And remember that, war is never peaceful.

Stressful person is emotional. He is living under constant pressures thus his mind remains blocked. Any person with a blocked mind always lacks vision and can only take short-term decisions.

Under these circumstances the fluctuations happen in the job or the business strategies and losses come as an unwanted guests.

"Can you afford to have stress?", is a billion dollar question. And there is one and the only answer. Certainly not. You must be a person of vision. Feel within yourself:

A Zero Stress Individual?

Further to have a deeper understanding, get the clarity that darkness is only absence of light. You can not fight with darkness. Just bring light in and the darkness disappears. Hunger is only absence of food. You can not fight with hunger. Just have food and the hunger disappears.

Confusion is only absence of clarity. You can not fight with confusion. Just get clarity and the confusion disappears. Poverty is only absence of riches. You can not fight with poverty. Just earn money and the poverty disappears.

Problem is only absence of solution. You can not fight with problem. Find solution and problem disappears.

Same way You Can Not Fight With Stress

<u>STRESS</u>

is only Absence of A Winning Strategy

Adopt "Winning Strategy For Success" and Your Stress Automatically Disappears

Human life by itself, is neither negative a positive. It is full of situations and situations. The situations which look unmanageable are normally referred to as problems.

Problem is not the situations itself but its consequences in your imagination. The negative feeling building up in your imagination in high magnitude is understood as fear while the mild fear is popularly known as worry.

The worry is building up pressure on the body and mind called as stress. The effect of stress on body is called as strain and on mind is called as tension.

When you manage the prevailing situation then managing stress is irrelevant so:

And Stress Stands
ERADICATED

People normally keep on focussing to learn something new. They want to learn all the methods for doing a thing and attempt to live them all.

It is not possible to earn money through illegal, immoral and unethical ways and at the same time claim within to live the opposite.

Stressful life style and living a stress-free life are the contrasts. Both can not be lived at the same time and by the same individual. You must select your choice and prepare yourself accordingly.

It is essential to unlearn the unwanted so that the desired and required can find a comfortable place to fit in. And the focus in life is not to keep on learning but:

Learn To Unlearn The Stressful Habits

<u>And</u>

Learn To Develop On The Relevant Ones

When you treat any life situation as a problem it start giving the reflections of complications and sufferings. You start feeling and imagining negative and negative starts happening.

Infact any problem is no problem. As already discussed in the book the so called problem is either a compliment on the competence gained in the past and is a matter to feel honoured or it is an opportunity to develop further competence for the future for which you are thankful.

The need is to initiate your STEP towards the most powerful STEP which is easy-to-understand and practical-to-implement.

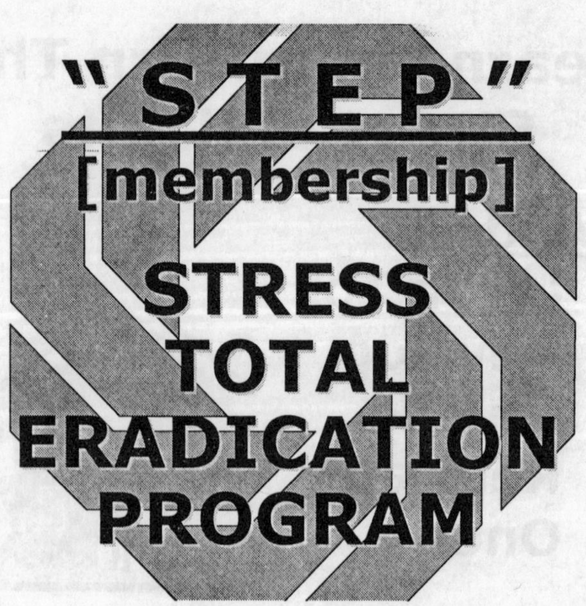

Members' Privilege

Group Session For Three Days On "Stress Eradication Through Samarpan Yog"

AND

Needbased Interaction Through Individual Sessions Or Website

www.stresseradication.com

As And When Any Unmanageable Situation Arises

There is a very old saying, "Nip the evil in the bud" which holds so true even today. Equally true is "A stitch in time saves nine".

To begin with the individuals get a conceptual understanding on how to live a stress-free life and then they have the rightful opportunity to have a need-based interaction.

When any situation which can get converted into stress is managed at the very initial stage, the stress will never be experienced by that individual and he will be living a stress-free life.

STEP is an investment for the generations to come for living a highly successful life along with peace and happiness.

The Key Is Not To Prioritize Your Schedule,

BUT TO SCHEDULE YOUR PRIORITIES

"STRESS ERADICATION THROUGH SAMARPAN YOG"

A unique and compact corporate program on Team Building, Leadership, Motivation, Time Management Mind Control and Stress Eradication.

Aim

In today's complex work environment, the key executives have limited time energy and resources to manage demanding situations. The energy is unnecessarily diverted in an attempt to manage the situation with arguments rather than investing it, with logic based clarity to enhance productivity and profitability. It is found that one of the important reasons for these unmanageable situations is the lack of a spiritual dimension of the scientific way of management. The need is to develop a system of integrated team operations by which you can acquire a unique ability to share correct and relevant information in a strategic way so that your TARGETED SUCCESS JUST HAPPENS.

Considering the growing needs of the key executives who aim to live success in this globally competitive environment, we have researched and designed an easy-to-understand and practical-to-implement STEP (Stress Total Eradication Program) which includes three days group sessions on "Stress Eradication Through Samarpan Yog" followed by Need-based Interaction Through Individual Sessions Or Website www.stresseradication.com as and when any unmanageable situation arises. The key executives must have a practical understanding of the respective winning strategy in all those situations where effective management of human and business relations is required.

A Journey of A Thousand Miles Begins With But A Single STEP

Benefits To The Participants

After attending the program, most participants will be able to:

- Learn the technique to program their inner mind for achieving success in day-to-day and long-term responsibilities.
- To arrive at win-win situation even with the troublesome people by maintaining harmony at both the ends.
- Develop an understanding about the logical control system for planning respective winning strategies.
- Learn the technique to relax when multi-directional thoughts are disturbing their mental balance.
- Open the door to live a quality life by understanding and deciding not to worry and feel tense upon irrelevant issues.
- Plan time to their best advantage and have more time at their disposal to takeover higher responsibilities.
- Develop an understanding to unlearn all the irrelevant concepts in practice.
- Feel command over most of their personal and corporate situations.
- Get clarity in establishing a practical link between spiritual values and successful management in various life situations.
- Learn on how to live a STRESS-FREE life.

Benefits To The Organization

- Enhanced productivity and profitability.
- Team's collective and harmonious contribution to the fulfillment of the corporate goals.
- Enhanced image within and outside the organization.

Methodology

- Case Studies
- Role Plays
- Situational Expressions
- Open Interaction
- Group Discussions
- Management Games

It's Not Stress That Kills A Person

It Is One's Reaction To It

CONTENTS

Day One

Vision For Success
Multiply In Business
Power Of Samarpan Yog
Switch "Off & On" The Mind
Merger of Individual & Corporate Goals

Day Two

Explosion Of Insult
Strategy To Win
Beyond Sincerity
Planning Time For Success
Living A Stress Free Life

Day Three

Closeness v/s Distance (A Delicate Balance)
Motivation Through Reprimand
Utilizing Mind's Spare Capacity
Practising 100% Concentration
Personal Action Plan

Days Four & Five

Individual interactive sessions to enable the participants develop understanding as per their specific situation. This way they feel confident to plan their own winning strategy and practically live success along with peace and happiness. Duration: 40 minutes per participant.